To Jean

With love and best
wishes from the
little boy who lived
next door !

Mike
xx.

21.5.15

COLLECTED POEMS

Also by Michael James Cook

POETRY

Stepping Stones
Reflecting In The Sun
Of Faith And Fortune
O Didaskalos

NON-FICTION

Have You Ever Thought?

Collected Poems

1959-2014

Michael James Cook

Matador
9 Priory Business Park
Kibworth Beauchamp
Leicestershire LE8 0RX, UK
Tel: (+44) 116 279 2299
Fax: (+44) 116 279 2277
Email: books@troubador.co.uk
Web: www.troubador.co.uk/matador

ISBN 978 1784622 404

British Library Cataloguing in Publication Data.
A catalogue record for this book is available from the British Library.

Printed and bound in the UK by TJ International, Padstow, Cornwall
Typeset in Aldine401 BT Roman by Troubador Publishing Ltd

Matador is an imprint of Troubador Publishing Ltd

This latest and probably last collection of my poetry is dedicated to my wife, Marjorie, whose love and care have kept me going through good times and bad since the day we met in 1959. That day changed my life for ever.

CONTENTS

"Velis et Remis"

INTRODUCTION

If I am honest I am not a great lover of poetry per se and never have been. When I was a promising footballer and cricketer with a professional career ahead of me I much preferred to play than watch. Likewise with poetry, I much prefer to write poetry than to read the poetry of others. I love the challenge of writing a poem about any subject in any given verse form in any mode. If I waited for inspiration I would never write anything. The inspiration kicks in along the way.

I wrote my first poem at the age of seventeen and have written hundreds since, over the past fifty-five years. The poem was entitled "Alone, Reflecting In The Sun" and is included in this selection. I wrote it for a fifteen year old girl I had recently met on holiday in Scarborough. We were both still at school and living at home; me in Stockport, she in Newcastle upon Tyne. I had earlier been told by specialists that my knee injury was so serious I would never play again. For me, writing poetry became very therapeutic. It came as a great surprise considering I failed English O Level at the first attempt. The girl later became my wife and we have been married now for over fifty years.

I have never believed that poetry should ever be in any way elitist. Its early use was by the great teachers of old who used it as a teaching tool by using rhyming couplets in whatever language they spoke, to impart knowledge to their listeners, most of whom could not read or write. It made it easier for listeners to remember (eg. Jesus of Nazareth and The Sermon On The Mount). I am not a poet; though I write poetry I do not earn a living from it. Over the years as a teacher I have used poetry a lot as a teaching aid. It has been very satisfying to know that many of my teaching colleagues and contemporaries (including Charles Causley, the famous Cornish poet and teacher) have used many of my poems and a few of my songs to good effect.

The poems for this collection were selected with a view to providing something for everyone, young and old alike; something old, something new, and something blue (just a few!). Some of the poems have been revised and reworked many times over the years. I am never entirely satisfied with the end product. A poem is similar to a painting and is a matter of personal choice whether it is liked or not. Like a photo without a caption it will mean different things to different people; sometimes more, sometimes less, than the poet intended. I hope the reader will find the collection enjoyable and useful.

For students of the art, the collection contains examples of many rhyming and non-rhyming verse forms, including Obsessive form (eg Sacred Mushroom); Concrete poetry (Getting Nowhere); Terza rima (Blow It); Hymnal short measure (Spinster's Soliloquy); Haiku (Creation); Roundel (Western Man); Ballad (At Seahouses); Rondel (A Written Proposal); Rondeau (Ricky); Pantoum (Weeping Willow); Tanka (The Way); Limerick (Bluebells); Sonnet (A Sonnet To Adam); Clerihew (If Music Be The…); Triolet (To Tell The Truth); Ballade (A Ballade Of The Sea); Cinquain (Worms) etc.

This collection came about because I am running out of steam. I am not getting any younger and I wanted to leave a legacy for my loved ones; family and friends, before it is too late. This is it, so I hope my labours have not been in vain.

Michael James Cook
Hinckley
2015

ALONE, REFLECTING IN THE SUN

If you could only be with me this moment and the more
To share this peaceful hour but for a little while.
To stop and rest and think; it is worthwhile.
To reflect, to recollect, and then to pass a smile.....
Some things well remembered and others best forgot:
The things we ought to do, the things we ought not.
To think a little time of nature and of life,
And the reason and the purpose we participate in strife.
Each day we live to encounter good and bad;
Some things make us happy and others make us sad.
Is this for nought or is there sense in all?
Is there an end and does man live to fall?
Each individual, born to make the choice between
Belief, or disbelief, as it may seem
To him or her who thinks of these and other things,
From whence our hearts be heavy or may sing.
And when we die, what then; are we but waste?
All knowledge stored in life to rot in but a buried place?
No use, no aim, no after-death, no life to come?
We are alive this peaceful hour,
Alone, reflecting in the sun.

QUESTIONS ABOUT LIFE

If there was no creation
Why do we create?

If there was no purpose
Why do we act with purpose?

If there was no reason
Why do we have reasons?

If there was no plan
Why do we make plans?

If there was no intelligence
Why do we use intelligence?

If nothing has value
Why do we worship?

If there was no image
Why do we imagine?

If there was no right or wrong
Why do we have conscience?

If there was no God
Why do we try to act like gods?

If there was no perfection
Why do we try to be perfect?

If there was no salvation
Why do we have faith, hope, and love?

If there was no after-life
Why do we go on living?

If there was no beginning
Why should there be an end?

If there was ever nothing
Why is there anything?

If life was an accident
Why isn't everything accidental?

If there was no choice
Why do we have freedom?

If there were no answers
Why are there so many questions?

HAIKU
(CREATION)

Change in a vacuum;
Something from nothing in space.
So what's the matter?

ODE TO THE UNIVERSE

Oh Universe, oh Universe
Your birth a mystery,
Will we ever learn your secrets
Or touch your majesty?

Oh Author of creation
Is there purpose in your mind?
Is the chaos accidental
Or the order by design?

Oh creatures of creation
Have you a mind to care?
Does it matter what is matter,
So long as it is there?

Oh Universe I learn of you
Through pupils in my eyes.
Your flashing beauty light I view
Through windows in the sky.

A speck upon a speck of dust;
Islands in seas of space.
I doubt if ever nothing was
Or else this world be waste.

ON BEING HUMAN

Oh Great Designer in the sky
May I ask the question Why?
When you devised the means
By which we propagate our genes,
Were you not entirely sober?
Or suffering a hangover?
It's a comical process which starts
I must confess, in physical farce.
Alas it ends in pointless pain.
Birth is messy, uncomfortable, a strain;
Agony for Mum and harrowing for Dad.
Potentially dangerous. You must be mad!
Was there really no other way
To secure our human progeny?

Unstable and many would say unsafe,
Our home is a planet with tectonic plates;
Volcanic eruptions, earthquakes and floods
(All provided by the One who loves?)
Shifting like sand deciding our fates.
Is this what's best for the human race?
When God made the Earth, He said it was good,
Yet most would rebuild it, if only they could.
We seek out cures for our social ills
And push the limits of medical skills.
For everything there is a time and place;
Maybe like nomads we are meant to roam
And secure ourselves a safer home
Somewhere out there in boundless space.

WHO IS LIKE THE LORD?

Muslims, Christians, Jews,
Monotheists everywhere,
Call me Yahweh, Allah, God
And drive me to despair.
We are all the same.
No need to choose -
But if I were your Creator
I would tell you now, not later,
That fighting over who is right or wrong
Is wrong and wrong and wrong.
What kind of deity am I
Who let's you live with blinkered eye?
I did not create so you could kill.
You have misunderstood my will.
You are meant to love instead of hate.
Therein lies **your** ultimate Fate.
Wise up and put your arms away
And fill the world with peace today.
If you **really** want to worship me
Then learn to live in harmony.

LOVE

Love is more than kinship,
Love is more than companionship.
Love is growing togetherness,
Love is knowing madness;
Love is in the mind,
Love is blind.

Love is more than lusting,
Love is more than trusting,
Love is meeting needs.
Love is shown in deeds;
Love is in the giving,
Love is living.

Love is more than demanding,
Love is more than understanding,
Love is needing each other;
Love is being another.
Love is in the sharing,
Love is caring,

Love is.

THE POTTER

The potter's wheel spins;
The potter in control
Moulds the clay
Gently with his hands
Giving form to shapes
Within his mind.

His mind, his hands, his wheel,
Work in unison,
In concentrated effort,
Developing skills to create
Precision and perfection
Out of nothing.

The potter is a useful being;
He helps us to see ourselves.
We too could imitate the potter
In motive, effort and deed;
Not making pots, but peace
And order out of chaos.

STARS

Stars are suns in the night.
Some are dead and some are bright.
They twinkle in the sky and give it light.
They offer hope of other forms of life.

The stars are company to our own,
In a universe which is our home,
Where we one day might freely roam.
Without them we'd be lonely and alone.

In billions of years our sun will die,
The human race will have to fly;
If all our hopes are to survive,
We need those suns to keep us starry-eyed.

ACTIONS SPEAK

Love and care are more oft caught
Than by some formal lesson taught.
Where principle and practise meet
The paradigm makes life more sweet.

DUTY BOUND

No worse love than duty;
To care for
But not adore,
To look after
Without laughter,
To give
And not live.
The receiver
Is not the deceiver.
"Duty Bound"
Makes a hollow sound;
Even to those who are well
It can seem an emotional hell.

CARE

It is too easy to say "we care"
From the comfort of an armchair.
Anyone can "care about",
Even the most common lout.
At a distance conscience pangs
Are smothered by more urgent plans.
It is a lie to say "we care"
When we are not actually there.
Loving activates the will to do
Whatever caring must be done.
It costs us time and effort too -
Committed "caring for" someone.

DO YOU CARE?

Do you care when you love me?
Or do you want to
Use me and abuse me
And tear me to pieces
Then cast me aside,
Leaving me to pull myself together
Later on,
And carry on
As if it hadn't happened?

A Sonnet To Adam

Before shadowy dawn I made a vow
To pay the debts of time, and needs repair.
Alone, I heard my lies denote despair;
Today, the voice of conscience takes a bow.
The stage is set to make amends from now
And players all assembled more aware,
Prepare the scene to end a Grande Affaire.
Insight: a curtain, slowly drawn somehow;
I touch your arm, an old reminder sign,
To draw attention more to what's in hand.
I must confess a frailty found in Man;
As Eve in Eden once betrayed her line,
The Fall is played again in every land.
Enjoy the fruits of love as best you can.

A Bad Start

Waning
Moonshine
On the newborn babe.
Wednesday's child,
Full of woe,
Born on an ebb tide
At sunset,
Will not have far to go.

Baby Talk

See your fingers
See your toes
Watch them vanish
Up your nose.

See your handies
See them meet
Watch them walk off
With your feet.

BLUEBELLS

Oh bluebells you're so beautiful,
Your abundance is reputable.
My baby daughter
Treats you like water
And wades in shouting
"Bluetiful".

LITTLE CHILDREN

Children live in a fantasy world
Of red-eyed monsters
Which come and eat them up
In the night;
Of good fairies
Who collect extracted teeth
And leave some money behind.

Children play at Shops, Doctors and Nurses,
And Mummies and Daddies;
Imitating and reliving experiences
They have known
Or have seen.
They live in a world of adventure
Copying all that they find.

Children live in fear of the dark
Without knowing why;
Of shapes and shadows cast
Upon the wall;
Of strange noises,
Exaggerated by the silence,
Heard in the middle of the night.

Children live in a world of make-believe,
Where everything wrong
Can be made to be right;
Where wishes
All come true.
They pretend to be people they are not
And dress up to suit the occasion.

Children accept what they are taught
Without question;
And are so conditioned by
Mummy and Daddy
And Teacher at school
(Who are fountains of truth to them)
To believe that adults are always right.

Children think that real people are not bad
And that all life is good.
Only witches, ghosts and dragons
Can do evil.
Yet they can be
Cruel to each other without caring,
And ignorant of how and why.

Children love their pets of all kinds,
From horses to dogs.
They love colours and sounds.
They believe in Jesus,
God and Father Christmas,
Like little angels, who when it suits,
Can become little devils.

Children take the world for granted
As if it all belongs to them.
As they grow older the dreams
Begin to fade.
They see it as it really is
And are disillusioned by its imperfections,
Wishing all their childhood dreams had been real.

FLIGHTS OF FANCY

When I was a child in infant school
Seated at my hard wooden desk
I was mesmerised by a spinning globe
Of places picturesque.

I never thought that I would see
Those far off lands and seas for real,
But now that world beyond the classroom door
Air travel has revealed.

Cape Verde Islands

Ten volcanic islands in a corral
Offer protection from attack,
As huge Atlantic rollers sap morale
Of sailors when they are beaten back.

A jewelled ring; such a dazzling sight
Sparkles in the tropical sun.
Snow white rippled sands reflect bright light
Amid shifting dunes the prudent shun.

Constant trade winds sway verdant palms
While azure skies and turquoise seas
Display their Afro-Caribbean charms
Urging all to cast off care and wander free.

A Daughter's Fright

Warm and cosy curled up in bed
She woke with a start and turned her head.
The bedroom door creaked slowly ajar,
A ghostly shadow crawled up the wall.
Cold fear shivered all down her spine
As she suppressed a plaintive whine.
Had a bogeyman come to call
Or a burglar to steal her toys?
She froze and stared wide eyed in fright
When suddenly all was bathed in light.
It wasn't a phantom or a spectre out to spook,
Only Daddy looking for his Puzzle book.

PARENTS "DELIGHT"

There was a young Cannibal called Gus
Who used to eat lettuce and stuff.
His parents said, "Son,
It's bad for your tum!
Why don't you eat humans like us?"

Gus thought for a time and made up his mind,
One had to be cruel to be kind.
"I'll do as you say
And eat meat from today"
Then he slew them both from behind.

EDUCATION

Parents in the land
Tell their kids to give a hand,
Get up, get out and earn some dough,
What do you think your education's for?
We want to get on and you should too;
Get up, get out and join the queue,
Join the rat race, get what you can,
Twist and steal and dodge the man.
Rent man, tally-man, papers to pay,
All by credit, day to day.
Everybody's doing it, all the nation:
Get what you can with education.

Teachers in the schools,
Teach their pupils all the rules.
Learn this, pass that, like A.B.C
Don't you know your education's free?
Swot all the facts to learn and learn,
Then one day you'll be able to earn,
Lots of money to spend and spend;
Money can buy you many a friend.
Keep on going from day to day,
Work hard, work fast, no time to play.
All the kids throughout the nation,
Get a good job with education.

Yobs and Dropouts all
Gather round my little stall.
Drugs and pills I have to sell,
Can't you see your education's hell?
Drives you mad with all the chore,
No social life, no life at all – it's all a bore.
Mum's at Bingo, Dad's not here –
Watching tele with a glass of beer.
No time to think, no time to pray,
God forgive us day to day:
All the people in all the nation,
Think again on Education.

School

A place of learning
Canned knowledge
Stuffed down your throat
Only to be spewed up
For exams and then forgotten.

A place of disciplining
The mind and body,
Having rules without the rod,
Where you can play up
And get out of anything.

A place of working
With irrelevant facts
And pointless information,
Killing interest and
Promoting boredom and ignorance.

A place of teaching
The end, not the beginning,
Of learning about
The unexplored boundaries
Of the world and oneself.

A place of thinking,
Where you are conditioned
To give the right answers
To all the wrong questions
About why you go to school.

A Lesson

"Line up properly.
Right
Girls first,
In you go.
Right boys
Follow on.
Stand up straight everyone,
That includes you Smith.
Sit down.
Quietly!
Take out your books.
Anyone not got a pen?
You'll need your rulers.
I want you to write what's on the board,
Copy it down
Neatly into your books.
Leave a margin.
Don't forget to underline
The heading and the date.
Today, as you can see
We are going to do
'FREEDOM'.
Keep your work tidy.
Remember what I said.
What's the matter Smith?
No pen?
For God's sake lad
Why do you always have to be different?
Here, use this one…
Now what's the matter Smith?

No ruler?
God give me strength!

Who hasn't finished yet?
Right. Good.
All, except you Smith.
Hurry up boy,
We can't wait all day for you.

Everyone finished.
At last!
Now, who can define freedom for me?…
Doing what you want?
Well, yes, up to a point.
Can anybody add anything to that?
Yes Smith?
What do you mean,
There is no such thing?

Let me explain –
Yes, I know that's the bell.
The bell is for me not you.
Now where were we…?
Oh well,
There isn't time to explain now.
Put your things away.
We'll carry on from here
Next week."

TEACHER

There was a teacher whose only concern
Was the number of passes his pupils could earn.
His reputation
Was their education,
But none of them learnt to love to learn.

SCHOOL CAT

She walks like a cat, aloof and sleek,
Seemingly soft, cuddly and vulnerable.
Her sharp eyes alert, catching every move;
Timid but wearing a face of stone.
This girl, in regulation blue, pads to school;
Shabby tiger, alley cat,
Carrying books beneath her arm, she purrs,
Warmed by thoughts of sensuous knowledge.
She comes for cupboard love, not to learn;
Attention like milk she laps up with hungry tongue;
She comes to take and not to give,
This earthy creature on the prowl for Tom.
At her desk she sits like Vesta in the hearth,
Body outstretched in lazy recline,
Waiting, watching over her domain,
Ready to pounce or snarl with arrogance
At some unsuspecting innocent who may disturb her peace.
This pampered pet with hidden claws of iron
Could tear out your heart
And watch the tears fall down your face,
Unmoved.

Towards A Just Society

No law can change the hearts of men
Nor put the world to rights;
Just educators know not when
Their pupils see the light.

Where unequal opportunities
And discouragements are rife,
We need a fairer share of inequalities
To supply just "tickets" for life.

Limitations

Amanda
The black and white Panda
Wants to fly like the Magpie.
Up she jumps
And down she thumps,
Then rubs her bumps with a sigh.
"Oh why can't I fly
Like the birds in the sky?
Do you think I'm foolish to try?"

FAME

There once was a tiger named Ezra
Who wanted to look like a zebra.
With paint black and white
He changed overnight
And became un tigre célèbre.

STUMPY MASCOT

Stumpy livens it up,
Stumpy spreads it around,
Singing and playing the Stumpy sound.

Stumpy is cuddly and cute to be with,
To hug him and kiss him is every girl's wish.
He's happy and playful all of the day.
He's a dream, he's a beauty,
What more can one say?

Stumpy jumps and shouts
With stumpy teeth in his stumpy mouth.
Stumpy stomps around
On stumpy legs on the bumpy ground.

Stumpy is stocky and true to his name.
To touch him and hold him is everyone's aim.
He's simple and honest, soft in the head.
He's a sight, he's a shorty,
What more can be said?

Stumpy is a short, fat, hairy being,
With short, fat, hairy legs.
His eyes light up to help him seeing
In the disco nights ahead.
There the Stumpy stumpers are found
Switching on to the Stumpy sound.

BLUE GUITAR

The winding howling twang
Of my guitar
Vibrates on a moonbeam
To the silent pockets
In your head
As it whines and it whines
Through the distant windows
Of your mind.
The echoes on a never-ending stream,
Gently floating and meeting
The rhythm of your heart-beat
With my guitar,
As it whines and it whines
Like a cat on a hot tin roof
Reluctant to leave
It's hopes behind.

IF MUSIC BE THE...

In virtuoso Vanessa-Mae
I see an exotic Take Away.
With her caramel skin, olive eyes and chestnut hair,
I want to eat her while she's playing there!

TAKE THE SUN

Take the morning sun
And fold it in your hand.
Take it with you when you go,
I'll keep the home fires burning.
You will see the seeds you sow
Growing in the land of learning.
Flower of youth so young
Shine forth out of the desert sand.
Unfold your petals and glow,
Satisfy your curious yearning.
When the heat has gone
And you're strong enough to stand,
You will fill the life-blood flow
With your experience and discerning.
Leaves will fall in autumn
As Nature does demand,
So take the sun and blow,
Before the winter comes in mourning.

I'm A Vandal

I'm a vandal,
I'm a wrecker,
I'm a breaker-in-two.
I'm a yobbo,
I'm a smasher,
I'm a nuisance to you.
I'm a wilful destroyer of beautiful things.

When I'm bored and frustrated
With nothing to do
I'll wander the streets
And get kicks with my feet
By mugging a woman or two.

When I'm tired and resentful
Of people like you,
I'll go with my mates
And get rid of my hate
By smashing a window or two.

When I'm scared and confused
By something that's true,
I'll carve out my name
And prove that I'm sane
By wrecking a car or two.

When I'm high and elated
By drinking a few,
I'll paint the town red
On blank walls like my head
By smearing a letter or two.

When I'm angry and violent
I'll damage what's new.
I'll skin a few cats
Or light fires with a match
And torch a building or two.

Whatever you state,
I'm proud to relate
I'M A VANDAL, mate!

To Dropouts Young And
Not So Young

Where do they hide from the
Hustle and bustle,
The pace, the race?
Do they dig pits
Lose their wits,
Escape by T.V.,
Or creep away in self-contained shells
To anonymous seas?
Do they take a trip
On the mainline,
To the sunshine
Glitter-litter-land of sham?
Poor people, puzzled people,
Tired people, bored people,
Apathetic stereotypes,
Waiting for something to happen.
Where's the spirit which won world wars?
Where's the drive, the zeal, the gall?
Is the wheel of change turning too fast?
Are they thrown by centrifugal force
Into some inert reality?
It is a tiresome wheel
Which turns and turns
Without oil or brawn,
In no particular direction.

So do something positive,
Please,
Before you are too old
To do anything at all
And drop out for good.

Soccer Girl

She's a true football fanatic
Everywhere you'll find her at it;
She'll give you a kick if you get in her way,
She'll boot the poor coach if he won't let her play
Football.

She'll play anywhere to get it,
People say she's 'energetic'.
If you want her to score just give her the ball,
Then hug her and kiss her and tell her it's called
"Football".

She's the queen of the soccer scene,
Superstar of her local team.
If you shoot her a line, she'll say she is game,
She'll always play ball if you mention the name
"Football".

Everyone thinks that she looks weird;
She's six foot six and sports a beard.
They all get a fright when she comes out to play
And run for their lives 'cause they think it is 'gay'
Football.

She's got FIFA in a whirl,
People call her "Georgie Girl".
She's the best in all the world.
She's appeared on tele with mud on her chest;
She's a female Pele, a Matthews and Best
Of all –
She's no boob with a ball!

GEORGIE

The people queued and gladly paid,
For Georgie was the best.
They could not understand his ways,
So anger they suppressed.

Poor Georgie kissed the girls and ran
From bed to bed to rest;
And Georgie satisfied his fans,
For Georgie was the best.

The best of Georgie was to come,
For Georgie was the best;
But Georgie felt that he was done
So gave football a rest.

He drank, he gambled, played the bore.
Poor Georgie blamed the press.
He stayed at home, then played abroad,
For Georgie was the best.

He sought a cure to gain some pride
For Georgie was the best.
He took a wife and tried to hide;
And gave the drink a rest.

Alas, he lapsed and beat his wife;
A drunkard at his best.
The surgeons tried to save his life:
George drank himself to death.

He could not cope with all the fame,
For Georgie was the best.
But in the end he made his name
Just being Georgie Best.

OFF-SIDE

A bastard.
Born out of wedlock,
My mother not a wife,
My father not a husband,
No legal rights.
Both too scared to commit,
Too selfish to make me legit.
I feel I want to hide;
It's as if they've scored a goal
And I've been ruled "Off-side".

UNITED

United scored and won the game.
Supporters cheered and waved their arms.
The players hugged and kissed and danced about,
But it still meant relegation.

Later, inside the changing room
When all the dirt and blood and sweat
Were washed away, the players dressed and
Each sat silently waiting.

The manager came in to give the news:
The Board of Directors had decided
That he and half the players would have to go.
United once, now divided.

NOT CRICKET

It wasn't cricket,
Thought the bowler
As he ran up to the crease
And bowled the last ball of the over.

He had finished with her –
Though he had made promises
And she was expecting his child.

"Over" shouted the umpire.
True,
Thought the bowler
As he continued playing the game.

The crowd of spectators applauded their idol –
He'd bowled another maiden over.

ON TOUR

You take my trust and tear it in two
By sundry secrets hidden from view.
You think I don't know but I do.

Blind eyes deny our numerous sins;
Subterfuge releases scorn with grins
Reflecting all our farcical whims.

Oh yes, I know what you're about.
I play the game myself. Have no doubt.
My aim is to keep the bond secure throughout.

A bubble bursts when you prick it;
Partnerships are like a game of cricket
Where neither side must take a wicket.

We battle to conjure up a score
As year by year we strive for more,
Until exhausted we declare a draw.

While I finish the innings with a final stroke
You can celebrate with a relaxing smoke.
Our tour is over and this game's a joke.

GAME

She beat you to me.
You had a lovely body –
Two arms and two legs,
But she also had a head,
Which crowns the lot,
Not just in Beetle Drive
But in the mating game.
My gain is your loss.
Remember that
Next time
The dice you toss.

ODDS ON STAKES

Two ate one
Four ate three
Six ate five
Seven ate nine.
What are the odds
On staying alive?
Two, four, six, seven, eight,
Who do we appreciate?
Eight might seem odd
Depending on the stakes.
All odds being even
I'd bet on lucky seven.

DURHAM REVISITED

Durham, sojourn like a game of chess;
From a poor pawn's plight to a castle's keep,
From a good knight's rest to a bishop's seat.
Probe, explore and ponder every door.

Find bed and board as an opening gambit,
Allowing easy movement and access
To the quaint old city's attractions
Which its buildings and narrow streets possess.

Founded by the monks of Lindisfarne
Who fled the Viking raiders of Holy Island
And took St.Cuthbert's body to safety inland
With their sacred relics and Gospels.

They settled on a tear-shaped peninsula
High above a crook-shaped bend in the Wear.
There the massive Norman cathedral stands
Marking the spot, awesome, without fear.

It houses the tomb of the Venerable Bede.
Yet after the battle of Dunbar
Scottish soldiers were imprisoned there;
Many died, their advance well checked.

The Castle, once home to the prince bishops:
Each had his own army, coinage, courts and crest;
Noble rulers of a palatinate,
Their limitless powers had to be checked.

Descend the majestic promontory
To the wooded inner bank, quite near,
And stroll to the old mill by the weir,
Now home to ancient Durham artefacts.

On Wednesday afternoons, school and college
Coxless pairs, and fours and eights, are stretched
Out on the river to Prebend's Bridge,
Where both crews and boats are checked.

Walk the outer bank of the river's crook
From bridges Elvet to Framwelgate.
Enjoy the very finest views to date,
Amble on to shops and pubs and Market Square.

Moving on past Claypath ascend the Gilesgate hill,
Turn right and drop down to the towpath.
Student regattas and long romantic triests;
Nostalgic memories strewn along the footpath.

Boathouses, colleges of Academia,
The old racecourse and sports ground, ever green;
The famous Durham Miners Gala scenes;
Old images, new ones keep in check.

Out to the west lies the railway station;
London to Edinburgh, East Coast Main Line.
Adjacent, the soaring viaduct holds
A signal, where trains are checked sometimes.

Above the station stands Wharton Park;
A terraced area with panoramic views
Across the whole city in all its hues.
The park boasts its own castle-shaped folly.

Finally, before you leave this place,
Before checking out of your hotel,
Remember, some people find chess is ace
While others find it hell.
So whether or not you play,
Don't forget to pay
The old fashioned way
By cheque
Mate!

At The Silver Blades Ice-Rink
(Bristol)

Swirling figures in cold air
Sliding and gliding
Gracefully
Over the crispy surface
Of the hard ice.

Packs of people pick their way
Stumbling and tumbling
Seemingly
In a frenzied dance-like trance
Anti-clockwise.

Steel silver blades underfoot
Swishing and hissing
Constantly
Cutting round the glassy rink
Menacingly.

Occasional spills of blood
Slipping and tipping
Carelessly
With splinters of brittle bone
Cracked on impact.

SAILING

I went for a trip on a sailing ship
And I thought I caught a glimpse
Of the water waving
As we tacked to and fro
Through the rain and the snow
Towards our haven.

We bobbed and bore towards the shore,
Full speed ahead we led the way.
The waves jostled and climbed
Like crowds of supporters
Urging us on with their roars
To an imaginary finishing line.

MY LOVELY MAIDEN

She was my lovely maiden
Whose eyes were bright as pearls.
She was my lovely maiden
Who loved the deep blue sea,
But now she is in heaven,
A place I'll never be.
She was my lovely maiden
And she was good for me.

My heart is heavy laden,
My eyes they smart with tears.
My heart is heavy laden
Now she has gone from me.
She didn't mind the weather
And she was lost at sea.
My heart is heavy laden,
Our love now cannot be.

We tried to find a haven,
Our hearts were filled with fear.
We tried to find a haven,
Her end it was to be;
For we sailed away together
Then waves swept her from me.
We tried to find a haven,
Her haven was the sea.

A Ballade Of The Sea

Paragon of power, the pundits say,
Your breathing causes waves to rise and fall.
People run to greet you shouting "Hurray"
But your swift embrace can become a maul
And the kiss of death awaits one and all.
Your beauty is deceptive; blue is grey.
Standard colours of tyrants always pall;
You will not have your way with me today.

Tempestuous lover enticing and gay,
Tempting your victims from behind your shawl,
Leading both young and old alike astray.
There are suckers at every market stall
And you, old-timer with your loathsome gall
Give licence to travel and right of way
To any who ask it, both great and small;
You will not have your way with me today.

There is nothing for which we do not pay.
You foam at the mouth when angry in squall
And your frothy tongue licks round every bay.
Hard rugged rocks and coastlines form a wall,
Hence to be washed away, however tall;
Homes, ships, lives of people at work and play.
But I am not to be part of your haul,
You will not have your way with me today.

Envoi

Sea, I can hear your terrible hunger call;
The rumbling in your belly as you sway.
Yes, even I can touch you when you crawl.
You will not have your way with me today.

A SHIP DIES

A ship, a wreck upon the heavy seas
Floats helpless, empty, all alone.
Buffeted by mountainous waves it reels
From side to side, heading for home.

The wind whistles round the mast
And clouds of spray fly past the bridge.
Her sides are gashed, she's sinking fast;
This ship, iced-up like a giant-sized fridge.

The Arctic waters, grey with gloom,
Rise and fall in rhythmic motion,
Beating out a warning of impending doom.
The ship, still flooding, lies lower in the ocean.

The icebergs, like an angry mob, hold back,
Watching as their victim slowly dies.
The ship, abandoned, lonely, painted black,
Smoothly slides beneath the waves without a sigh.

The Fishermen Of Caldey

We went to see the dropouts
On the Isle of Caldey.
Some of them were holy
And others had simply
Dropped in for the day.

We went by boat from Tenby
The "fishermen" to see.
While some caught fish at sea,
Others were on dry land,
Odd- men-out making scent.

We landed at the slipway
And spied some loaves of bread.
Some people went well-fed,
Food provided daily,
While others elsewhere starved.

We entered the island shop,
Packed full of souvenirs
And gifts to ward off fears.
The scent sold like hot cakes;
A new brand 'Bread of Life'.

The Christians were all trading
Selling their wares for cash.
The House of God won't last,
Coining money like a mint,
As in the Temple yard.

We visited the lighthouse.
The keepers all were gone.
No shining light was on.
No one to show the way.
The monks were all at prayer.

I entered the monastery
Seeking spiritual life.
I couldn't take my wife;
Women were excluded.
I felt that way within.

The monks take vows of silence,
Obedience and chastity;
A cloistered fraternity
With masochistic needs
Hidden behind closed doors.

We left the Isle of Caldey,
Our pilgrimage was done.
Refreshment, we found none.
Where were those "fishermen",
Not catching fish but men,
Who served the Holy One?

DRIFTING AWAY

You are drifting away from me
Like a boat which has lost its mooring,
Slowly, almost unseen,
Undulating with the water,
Receding, soundlessly.

Your mind vacillating, uncertain,
Lost in a dilemma:
Who to have, what to do,
Who to hurt –
Them, me or you?

With your loving you have created hatred.
With your demanding
You have deprived
Even those you love
Of a lifeline to cling to.

DESERTED ISLE

Milky sand slurped by lethargic waves
On a silk-soft carpet beach of foam.
Footsteps fast fading from the water's edge
Landward-bound, seeking a home.
Both of us abandoned on a deserted isle,
Shaded only by the sword-blade leaves of palms.
Eye-pools reflect the twinkling sun on sea.
Castaways, love-loose in each other's arms;
Open mouths word seashell sentiments,
Broken only by the taunting breeze.
Bloated lips suck in the salty air.
Entwined we stand on shifting sand.
Overhead, anvil shaped thunder clouds rise in haste,
Poised to lash vengeance on an ocean wasteland.

An Island Experience

There was a time when passion made my stomach
Do a somersault;
When aching limbs and throbbing heart
Made fire within my soul.
But now the ticks of time have slowed me down
And worn away the fuse to blow me up inside;
So now I know that I am growing old.
The uncertainty of youth
Which once could cause distress
Has grown to be a steady anchor in the waters
Of my decaying prime.
Like a boat long-moored, which breaks up and rots,
Its timbers floating on a wearing sea no tide can stop,
I'm helpless but at one with time.

That sure footed arrogance peculiar to youth
Which helped me climb the highest cliffs
Whose rocks were thousands of millions of times
Older than myself;
Which made me think I could compete with Nature
And succeed;
To conquer all, I understand,
Was just an ego-tripping cry for help,
Desperate to prove myself a man.

The rocks and sea will still be here when I am gone.
Now I must learn to crawl back to the sea.
No further hope of being washed up on the shore.
No wasted dreams to tie me any more,
For I am conquered by the One Who gave me birth.
This island home I must desert
On a one-way trip, never to return.
I kiss the rocks goodbye.

The Islands Of Men

There are islands of men
There are oceans of love
And peace in the sky
Up above.
There are soldiers of sand
There are bombs made of snow
Washed up on the shore
Down below.
The islands of men
With their soldiers of sand
Keep growing each day
Till the winds come and blow them all away.

There are islands of men
There are mountains of hate
And war for a meal
On a plate.
There are houses of flesh
There are birds made of steel
Caught up in the fire
Of ideals.
The islands of men
With their houses of flesh
Keep rising each day
Till the flames come and burn them all away.

There are islands of men
There are rivers of greed
And dust in the air
That we breathe.
There are temples of sin,
There are gods made of clay
Built up from a pile
Of decay.
The islands of men
With their temples of sin
Keep falling each day
Till the seas come and wash them all away.

There are islands of men
There are babies of hope
And faith in the sails
Of their boats.
There are cargoes of salt
There are seas made of earth
Spread over the land
Of our birth.
The islands of men
With their cargoes of salt
Keep sailing each day
To a port which is never far away.

AT SEAHOUSES

Seahouses, grey and so damp did seem
And dark were the islands of Farne.
The waves lay calm but the seagulls screamed
And still was the air with alarm.

The morning mist o'er the sea did rise
And pale shone the watery sun.
The time had come for the seals to die
And cold were the hearts of our young.

The fishermen in their boats stood proud
But sad were the eyes of my son.
Policemen came to control the crowds
Who cried that the deed be not done.

Then the marksmen with their guns held tight
Went out on the ebb of the tide.
Their shots rang out and the seals took fright,
For them there was no place to hide.

Three thousand seals, grey and white, lay dead
And gone was their watery calm.
Their blood flowed quick and the sea turned red
And black were the clouds over Farne.

TIME AND TIDE

At an ebbing three score years and ten
I have become a man of easy tears.
My approaching death, not if but when
Makes me mourn the loss of future years.
My loved ones may miss me, more than I them,
For I shall have shed all human fears
No longer swayed by the tides of men.

At Lyme Regis

As we strolled along the promenade at Lyme
We watched the raging sea below.
We felt the waves of passion rise and fall
Knowing our time would ebb and flow.

The stars like windows slowly hidden
By curtains of cloud, silently drawn
Across the sky by some invisible hand,
Kept us apart as we tried to keep warm.

As we looked out across the Bay
The lighthouse flashed its warning with its light.
We kept our distance like the ships at sea,
Taking care to sail a course we knew to be right.

We played with ideas to breach the gap
As we ambled side by side, not touching.
Giddy words danced across our lips
And we laughed at silly pointless things.

Our thoughts were in turmoil like the waters below
And our minds cut off from those around;
Like pebbles thrown up in a mass of spray
We hoped there was a haven to be found.

Did we think we could survive like the dinosaurs?
Would we stand together and never suffer loss?
Hand in hand and cheek to cheek we faced the open sea.
Come the day of reckoning, could we ever count the cost?

As we peered into the harbour from the Cobb,
The deep black water lapped along the wall.
Did you sense the heartbeat racing in my breast?
Did you hear my stifled, anguished mating call?

Can you share the depths of my emotions?
Are your moods in harmony with mine?
When I touch you do you tremble?
Can you walk the pathways of my mind?

As we made our way back to the car on foot
Retracing steps we'd taken earlier on,
We shared the moment of a lifetime
Wondering whether we should carry on.

PERSPECTIVE

How far is a metre
To a snail?
How high is a hill
To an ant?
How great is a man
Compared to the Earth?
How small is our planet
Against the sun?
What size the sun
Compared to our galaxy,
In which there are at least
A hundred thousand million others?
What size our galaxy
In the vast universe
Containing millions of other Milky Ways?
All parts must go
In proportion to the Whole,
And we, a part,
Must find our own
Perspective.

The Story Of The Dinosaurs

Before the orogenesis
Of the Alps and Andes;
Before the Himalayas,
Rockies and Pyrenees
Folded into the blue sky;
Before Man had his birth
And wrote his name in the sand,
Dinosaurs ruled the Earth.

The Book of Earth History
Four thousand six hundred
Pages, a million years long,
Leaves a lot to be read.
The dinosaurs fill some
One hundred and thirty
While mere Man appears
On the last page only.

Humans never saw their success
Nor witnessed the decline
Of these lords of creation.
In their Triassic prime
They straddled the shrinking globe
In majestic splendour,
Dominating continents,
Paragons of power.

Elite of the Reptile Age,
With egg-brains at their core,
Two-footed and four-footed

Carnivores and herbivores;
Horned, spiked, long-necked, duck-billed,
Large, medium and small.
Some monsters walked upright.
Some crawled on all fours.

The Mesozoic era
Of prehistoric beasts,
Gave pride of place to tyrants
In tropical world heat.
Terrible lizards roaming
Upland, swamp and jungle;
Swimmers, diggers, tree-climbers,
Tearing Earth asunder.

A two-legged meat eater,
Awful Allosaurus,
Swept Jurassic landscapes
Hunting Brontosaurus.
Theropod of theropods,
Tyrannosaurus Rex,
King killer of Cretaceous,
A cannibal, came next.

Sounds of brawn reverberant
Rumbled beneath the ground,
Like distant thunder coming
When these giants roamed around;
Cold-blooded automatons
Who killed without a care.
The modern bear and lion
Are harmless dwarfs, compared.

T.Rex, with mouth a metre wide,
Armed with scimitar-teeth
And hands hooked with tearing claws,
Was truly a masterpiece:
The ultimate in brute strength,
A tale of brawn triumphant
Over brain for generations,
Till victor lay defunct.

(Dinosaurs, oh dinosaurs,
Oh why are you extinct?
Was it racial senescence
Or did you never think?
Chromosomes in chaos
Producing toothless freaks?
Who preyed upon your eggs
And relatives did eat?
Did the climate grow too cold?
Were there epidemics?
Did your food supply all fold?
Were changes far too quick?)

Evolution has its failures.
The dinosaur was one.
Compared to the dinosaurs
Man is but Tom Thumb.
Should we ever be their peers
We need to survive
Another one hundred
And twenty-nine million years.

The Lizard

Soft undulating contours sloping to the sea,
Steep cliffs along the coastline edged with Serpentine.
A bleak and rugged landscape with scarcely a tree,
Windswept downs of gorse and ferns, people in their prime.

Dressed in drab stone houses, the village looks bare
And the lighthouse stands in sad isolation.
There is a natural beauty, which is quite rare
And the natives retain their proud insulation.

Heavy air induces lethargy and saps the will,
In sharp contrast to the tireless toil of the sea.
Jagged, polished, red-olive rocks crack along sills.
What a destructive soul the Atlantic can be!

The red in the rocks serves as warning to shipping;
Many wrecks lay at rest round this treacherous coast.
Smugglers of old did their trading and tripping
From well-hidden caves which harbour their ghosts.

Grockles are welcome to stay for a visit
But The Lizard is no place to come to settle.
It's a creature of habit and lazy with it;
If it shows a forked tongue, be on your mettle.

Constrictor Boa

There once was a boat builder, Noah,
Who docked for a Take-Away in Goa.
All those aboard ate chicken
And many creatures were stricken
By Delhi Belly, like Boa.

Ricky

My canine friend came from the vet.
We took him in without regret.
Alsatian-Collie cross was he;
A friendly dog we called 'Ricky'.

He licked my hands when we first met
And toured the garden in the wet,
Deciding that his home was set.
I swore to him he'd always be
                My canine friend.

Whenever left, he'd sit and fret
But proved a very faithful pet.
I took him walks in pastures free;
Their streams he used to jump with me.
I doubt if ever I'll forget
                My canine friend.

Puss Puss

She lay on the thick woollen pile
Of the carpet in front of the fire,
With her legs outstretched
And eyes half closed,
Waiting to be petted.
I knelt down beside the feline creature
So that I could touch her.
And with my palm I stroked
And caressed her silky hair,
Thinking "Oh, what a lovely pussy.
What a lovely pussy you are!"
She purred with contentment
Licking my hands,
Expressing her joy.
Later, she rose to leave the room,
Her lips half-open in a wicked smile.
And when she reached the door
She turned her head
And cast a knowing eye
In my direction.
Then, did I hear her sigh
And softly say
" Goodbye "?

MICKEY THE MONKEY

Mickey the Monkey
Lives in a tree.
He knows his numbers
One, two, three.

One for the monkey
Two for the tree.
Three for the letters
A.B.C.

Mickey the Monkey
Looks down on me.
He walked with angels
Out of the sea.

A is for ape-man
B is for me.
C is for cloning
One, two, three.

Mickey the Monkey
Can talk to me.
He told me the secret
Of Sirius B.

Was it a spaceman
Up in the tree?
Whence came the monkey
Came you and me?

WORMS

Devil's
Flesh ripple-ringed
Sent to work underground
Tunnels in tombs of dead silence
For good.

To search
Buried bodies
And eat away decay,
Swelling jelly-soft bellies for
Blackbirds.

BIRD PARADISE

Birds of Paradise
Caged in netted zoos,
Wired and snared
They lose their shine
And fade away in twos.

Faced with extinction
Herded together
Mated and paired
For their own good –
Never mind the weather!

Sad lifeless creatures
Lost in a strange land
Preserved for us
To pay to see –
Pound coins in captive hands.

SWAN SONG

Super Mute Swan with crooked neck
Sitting on her nest of down
Tied by the instinct to survive,
Swaddling her cygnets five.

And on the coiling wind
Echoes of a bass guitar
Belting sounds conveyed by currents of air
Across silent fields to animal ears elsewhere.

Noise like the beat of a soldier's drum
Hammering the brain, smothering thoughts,
Blotting out both fear and foe
Projected from the darkness of the disco.

When I succumb, the urge to sing
Electrifies notes in my throat.
Pray that my chords be not too long
Nor my song too strong for the Swan.

Food For Thought

The tits in the trees
Swayed on the branches
In the breeze.
Then finches came down
And pecked at the ground
Around the patio.
Then down swooped the
Blackbirds, robins and wrens.
They all sang their songs
As they came and they went,
Thinking only of food;
No sad lament
But gay and abandoned,
Expressing their joy.
I sat at the window
And gazed at the tits
As they bobbed up and down.

Then I remembered
Those breasts full and ripe.
The times I had sucked them
At noon and at night,
Giving me pleasure
And giving me life.
Food as a baby
I'd sought and I'd found
Blindly by instinct
At the nipple-go-round.
Like the birds full of insects
I'd taken my fill,
Then gurgled contentment
And later lay still.
Now that I'm older
The birds that I see
Give food for my thoughts
Which are not on the tree.

TREE SPEECH

The dawn chorus is
A natural alarm clock
Of signs and signals.

The sound messages
Are the battle cries of birds
In choral warfare.

Communication
System with a limited
Vocabulary.

Reports about food,
Boundaries and moods, to mates
Waiting in the wings.

Each species' mating
Call, is a sound barrier
To inter-breeding.

Be not deluded,
Even by the twitter and
Charm of chaffinches.

The birds sing to birds
While we talk to cats, which oft
Regard us as trees.

Weeping Willow

Morning, afternoon and night,
Here I'm rooted to the spot.
Casting shadows in the light;
Weeping is my chosen lot.

Here I'm rooted to the spot,
In the garden at the front.
Weeping is my chosen lot.
When gales rage I bear the brunt.

In the garden at the front,
My arms reach down to touch the ground.
When gales rage I bear the brunt;
The only time I make a sound.

My arms reach down to touch the ground,
Making real my worldly fears.
The only time I make a sound,
I'm moved to mourn the passing years.

Making real my worldly fears
With every passing friend and foe,
I'm moved to mourn the passing years;
I stand and shed soft tears of woe.

I stand and shed soft tears of woe,
In silence weep sweet tears of joy
With every passing friend and foe,
For each new baby girl and boy.

CRYING

Whenever I cry
A hidden feeling is released
Which has been fermenting
Inside my being
And bubbled over.

A part of living
Forbidden to be seen
Until it is considered
By others to be
The proper time and place.

When You Are Gone

When you are gone
It will be like the setting of the sun.
Time will stand still
And the days will be empty
And difficult to fill.
The heart strings, like cat gut, will be cut.
No love songs to play,
Only memories of melodies
And chords of harmony now passed away.

When you are gone
My world will be shattered like a broken vase.
Sounds will be silent
And sights will be blurred.
The tears will well up
And choke in my throat, gripped in grief.
Little things forgotten,
Brought to mind, remembered;
Sentiments of pity, pain and passion, once begotten.

When you are gone
Your kindness and consideration will be lost.
The sure protection
Which you freely gave
Will remain a debt
Impossible to repay this side of death.
Did you ever know
When your eyes kissed mine
How little time we had before you had to go?

When you are gone
I shall miss your quiet words and ways;
Your inner peace
Which gave me confidence;
Your tender touch
Which cared and calmed my troubled breast.
Your love will live on,
Like the warmth of the sun,
In me and mine, when you are gone.

A Bit Of Fun

As I lie here in the sun
I can dream about the one
Who has come to make my life
A bit of fun.

As I sit here in the shade,
I can dream about my trade
Which has made me millions from
My bit of fun.

As I lie here on the beach,
I can dream about the peach
Of a woman who provides
A bit of fun.

As I sit here facing South,
I can dream about the mouth
Which has truly granted me
My bit of fun.

As I lie here on the bed,
I can dream about the legs
Which have lain next to mine in
A bit of fun.

As I sit here in the raw,
I can dream about the bore
Who has always tried to spoil
My bit of fun.

Happy dreams
Which make my living
Gay and abandoned.
I'm resigned to enjoying
My little bit of fun.
In the sun
Or in the shade,
I've got it made
And I'm content,
To lie and dream
And set the scene
To film
My bit of fun.

In Love With My Car
(With apologies to Roger Taylor of Queen)

The machine is a dream
So clean,
With pistons pumping,
Hubcaps gleaming.
Holding the wheel
I steer with my hand
On the gear,
Throbbing with life
Racing along
In top.
Pulsating machine
Is well greased.
I've got a feel for my car
Like an obsession
And an addiction
Rolled into one.
It's a thrill
Driving my automobile.
Told my girl "goodbye"
For my four-wheeled friend
Never talks back
When I'm cruising in style,
Out to impress.

And later –
Cloth in hand,
I'm wiping it clean,
Gently polishing,
Caressing the sheen,
To mirror my face
In some masturbatory
Fantasy.
With my phallic symbol
I stand outside my door –
Steppenwolf would say
It was "For Ladies Only" –
Paying narcissistic homage.

IN A SPIN

My shoes are on my feet
And my feet are on the ground.
The ground is on the Earth
And the Earth is spinning round.
Round and round the sun we go,
The sun in turn is turning.
Moving on and on we blow
Through boundless worlds of space.
The shoes upon my feet will rot.
What end the traveller waits?

DRINK TO ME ONLY

I was a magnum
And you kept me to yourself.
Now you are a drunkard
And you've had your fill of me.

IN A BEER GARDEN

Summer days, heat haze,
Sipping cider through a silver straw.
Fizzy pop,non-stop,
Consumed with thirst as bubbles pop
And sweat drops
From members of a beer garden.

Prize prats, fancy hats,
Paraded by those poor enough to bore.
Cloth shades, hand made,
By odds and sods of every type,
Gather aimlessly
In the corners of a beer garden.

Shouted words, unheard,
Euphoric outbursts erupt with glee.
Cackles sharp, dogs bark,
Peeling flesh displayed on shrinking earth
Cracking cares apart
With bottle-toasting in a beer garden.

Red wine, mellow and mine,
In the bloodstream for a time.
Strong spirit run along
Quick enough to let me flee.
Shorts enough to get me home;
Ale aplenty do your duty,
Free the jailers and the jailed
In the confines of a beer garden.

Carve Up On The Motorway

Steel sharp razor cars
Cut into the soft blotchy flesh of fog.

Ahead,
Pimples of red light
Stand out like familiar features of a face.

Taught hands tightly grip
The instruments of life and death,
Skilfully guiding them with surgeon-like precision,
Tracing the outline of the hard shoulder.

Laser beams of light converge,
Peeling the layers of skin
(Some thick, some thin)
Before incision.

Accidentally,
Knives meet sharply
Deep down inside the body.
Pools of blood slowly congeal in the still air.
For a time the flow stops
And the arterial road remains blocked
By the resulting embolism.

THE CLOT, ST. MARGARET'S HOSPITAL, EPPING.

I remember the pain pulsating
With each sledgehammer blow
Against my chest –
And the panic
As I gulped for air
And coughed up lumps of blood
Instead.

It was night.
The ward was sleeping.
A single light
On the wall opposite
Cast shadows which were all a blur.
Out of time, floating,
Fragments of fact and fiction
Punctured projected images on my mind.
All I could hear
Was the soft hiss around my head
Of oxygen cylinders beside my bed.

At unknown intervals
I opened and closed my eyes.
Minutes? Hours? Days? Weeks? Months?
Maybe even years?
In and out of time
Dodging the random Reaper,
More by chance than design.

Conscious only of the mask about my face
And that slow continuous hiss
Of the pure life-saving gas
Travelling along some umbilical-like cord
From a placenta I could not turn my head to see.

My body racked, spread-eagled,
Feet slightly raised,
No pillow for my head,
Which spun confusingly
In a mist of uncertainty.

My lungs, blocked with clotted blood,
Heaved and strained, as in a tug-of-war,
To gain but whits of air.
Each gasp for breath
Choked in my throat
And gave a sense of drowning;
(where in the deep, the water fills you up
until you cannot take another drop,
but hit the bottom dead).
Sinking slowly into the dark
Unconscious depths of time and space
Once more
Wanting it to end.

Only to rise later,
Surfacing like some unsinkable cork.
Aware a night nurse posted by my bed
Lightly held my hand.
The Sister rearranged the mask
Around my face
And wiped away my tears and sweat.
A smattering of conversations overheard:
"Pulse rate one-forty…"
"…his family been informed?"
"Yes Sister…shall I change the bottle over?"
"…in the right thigh I think…"
"Relations flying down…should be here soon."
"Maximum number of mills…morphine…"
"…thank you nurse. The doctor's on his way."
"Pethidine…"

Fine flesh the needles stabbed like steel darts.
Punctured skin scabbed with blood…
The fight to save my life went on
With doctors reappearing.
Blood pressure count with pulse was checked
And record kept of breathing.
The pressure on my chest increased;
Crushed in a vice of granite rock
I could not move.
I waited for the final grip
To take its hold
And squeeze me,
Leave me,
Dead.

The night sped on.
I struggled in a stupor.
Whims and fancies filled my head
Of childhood days when all was red and rosy.
Alas my mind kept wandering.
Memories, as visions flashed by,
Brought back a sense of living.
Thoughts of home
And loved ones near and far
(I wished they could be nearer)
Became quite clear
And then would disappear.
I had a vision of my youth
As in some messy shorts and shirt
With muddy boots I scored a goal
And fell down in a puddle.

I slumped again into a state of bliss,
Oblivious to pain and suffering,
Knowing nothingness.
The night sped on
It's shadow hanging over me
As I hung on.
It dawned on me
If I should die –
Next second –
My loved ones would not know
And nor would I.
'Tis such a simple step
From one plane to the other.

And so it was I woke to find
The morning sun,
The crisis over
And the battle almost won
And all the fighters gone
Except for one;
Who lay as helpless as a new-born babe
Too weak to feed himself or raise his head,
With five more weeks to lie in bed
Before returning home.
The clot,
Anti-coagulated,
No more could stop
The rivers of life within.

BROKEN

I feel as if the depths of hell surround me;
I'm on my own and all alone and drowning.
If only you could know the pain I bear
You would not stop me killing care,
For all I want to do is sink into oblivion.
A deep sleep enfolds my body and at peace
I lie with limbs embalmed to be released
From life on earth, this living hell I know as home,
A place of darkness all my own
As in a coffin I wait to rot and turn to dust;
Or should the fires of hell confine me
Consumed by flames my flesh will smell
Then peal off to the bones to spell
A warning to those who wag their fingers in disgust.
I'm not the guilty one who planned this plot;
My life's no more my own than yours is not.
If only you could empathise and enter in
My mind and soul to dwell therein,
You would not want to share my lot:
The mocking voices of the people whom you cannot see,
Their laughter and their jokes, complacency
Abounds in all who do not understand.
I am to die, I know that now, there is no other way.
And you and yours will kneel and pray:
"There but for the grace of God, go I".
Your tears will fall upon my grave.

Your love, my life it could not save.
Then they will toil to dig a hole so big
That all the worms on earth may have their fill
As in the dirt my body and my soul lie still.
Despite the happiness life can give
I have no more the will to live.

A DAYTIME NIGHTMARE

Demons of the night be gone
I care not for your dance or song,
Of torments, endless and severe.

Dawn approaches, dreams depart.
I must awake and play my part,
Expecting nothing in return but fear.

The days are long and tedious,
Each one alikened to the previous.
No respite from the jeering crowds I hear.

Devils of the day return
To tempt me, but their 'tempts I spurn,
'Tho mocking laughter fills my ears.

The urge to self-destroy eats up my mind,
Devouring all other thoughts I find;
Slug-slow my brain, no longer clear.

Deny me not the right to live or die.
I care not for your reasons why
The scoffers scoff and lechers leer.

If I must suffer now for what I'm not,
What need of God? It's best forgot.
No need for mystics, prophets, seers.

In bed my dreams are on the run,
Racing hither and thither, no place to rest upon.
I'm wide awake and out of gear.

With head in hands I sit around,
The record plays but makes no sound.
My head now spins as visions reappear.

I cannot put the world to rights.
I cannot even sleep at nights.
I cannot even taste the bitterness of beer.

Outside, the tides of fortune rise and fall.
The waves of wonder, wide and tall
Smash and crash against the seaside pier.

And on a boat I float upon the sea.
The stranger on the shore I see – is me.
So far apart and yet so near.

I reach out and shout with all my voice.
It echoes, bellows, round the coast.
A ghostly silence chills the air, all noise has disappeared.

A solitary boat across the bay is sailing.
The weather's bright, but inside me it's raining.
The shallow land is flooded by my tears.

On an island of my own I stand and stare,
Surrounded by the traps I've set in my despair,
Impairing all my steps and those to whom I'm dear.

People watch me pace my cage
And like a lion roar, in silent rage.
No sympathy nor help, they keep well clear.

They cannot understand my state.
They tell me not to worry but it's too late;
My name upon the wall is just a smear.

I wish no harm to anyone upon this earth.
No hatred in my heart I hold, nor mirth.
All life to me is sacred and all things I revere.

No more poetic words I'll write,
I have no more the will to fight.
The demons of the night to me adhere
And I have reached my life's nadir.

Unto The Third Generation…

Megalomaniac son
Of a melancholic
Father
And a manic
Mother.
Brother
To a schizophrenic
And a neurotic
Sister.
Father
To a normal
Son?

Mind

Mind is clear, positive and creative;
Mind is confused and chaotic;
Mind is hidden, concealed inside.
Mind is negative and destructive;
Mind is alive and can kill.
Mind causes us to mind,
So mind we must our minds.

THE ELECTRO-CONVULSIVE THERAPY WALTZ

Take up your partners
For the melancholia waltz:
E.C.T., One – Two – Three,
E.C.T., One – Two – Three.

Patients behind high walls,
Plucked from depressing wards,
Pulled through glass swinging doors
Terrified of what's in store.

Enter the Waiting Room,
One person to a bed,
Screens veiling fear and gloom,
Here comes the old pre-med!

Atropine warms the blood,
Waiting so patiently.
Drug makes you feel so good,
Drifting so sleepily.

In a line, off we go,
Beds wheeled in one by one,
Charge nurse takes us in tow
To see which doctor's on.

Caste mark upon her brow,
Like the spot on T.V.,
Switched off I know not how,
Receding silently.

Teeth bite on rubber bone.
I'm counting: One – Two – Three,
Doc jabs the needle home,
Here comes the E.C.T.

Shocked rigid, counted out,
Body now in a fit.
Stiffened limbs shake about,
At the flick of a switch.

Meet myself coming round,
Aching jaw, thumping head.
Cups of tea lost and found
While I stir on the bed.

I will rant, I will rave:
"Save the next dance for me."
In a trance I will praise
E.C.T., One – Two – Three.

The Valley Of The Living Dead

As I walk through the valley of the living dead,
I see the blind who cannot see the light.
I watch the deaf who cannot hear the word.
I meet the dumb who cannot talk.
Having eyes to see and ears to hear and tongues to speak
They have not learned to use their senses,
So they dwell in the valley of the living dead.
Pathetic cases of their own creation
Gathering round their shallow souls
Material possessions to fill their lives.
All hopes are based on false elation
Manufactured to create sensation,
Only to find they are bent and broken
As they walk through the valley of the living dead.
The poet who has lost his rhyme,
The minstrel who has lost his song,
The preacher who has lost his faith,
All hope that someone else will lend a hand
When finding signs they do not understand.
The scientist who lacks imagination,
The proud who strive to keep their reputation,
All are walking through the valley of the living dead.
They know not why they live.
They work to buy their happiness,
All slaves to ownership.
They flaunt their artificial beauty
Which by money they possess,

Hoping all who view their gains will feel deprived
And like them, will want for more.
Yet all the time they are slowly dying
As they walk through the valley of the living dead.
People come and people go while time ticks on.
Some have a daughter, some a son.
From all the truths of life they run.
Ignorance multiplies their guilt;
Their minds they cannot mend,
Their love they cannot share,
Their hearts are empty, bare.
Colourless characters, eyes completely blank,
With naked personalities stand
Lined up in order hand in hand
Along the valley of the living dead.

Cut short my visit to this place
Where millions gather to perform
Their roles in life unto its end.
They live, yet all the time pretend
To be what they are not.
This confused and ugly lot
Are driving me insane.
Spare me the pain
To watch them rot
In the valley of the living dead.
Dear God, on whom I call,
I do not know you much at all.
I thought I did but then the darkness came
And clouded up my cluttered brain.
Why did you lead me to this place?
Was it to understand your grace?
Release me now and let me live.

The light is bright and crystal clear.
The mist inside my head is lifting.
My eyes are moist with joy,
My freedom now I will enjoy
And new found knowledge I'll employ
In helping those who do not use their senses
To appreciate the wonder of the world
Outside the valley of the living dead.

HOPE

Hope is a product of desire
A flame from a passionate fire
Flickering small or licking tall
The walls of kind or mal-intent.
Smouldering ashes, dreams destroyed,
Fanned by fluctuating gusts of wind
Ignite the debris of discontent
Which piled too high consumes within.

Hope has new horizon faces
To lighten the darkest places.
A dawn each day along each way
Alleviates depressing night;
A smile or encouraging word
From stranger or from passer-by,
A lighthouse beam, a flash of white
On stormy seas of black despair.

Hope is a traveller unpaid.
In time, a servant not a slave:
Cast in a spell in wishing well;
A footprint in the desert sand;
The sound of laughter far away;
An ambulance, a distress flare.
In times of stress a helping hand
Or a lifebuoy self-inflated.

Hope is a child of want which cries.
When pacified it slowly dies.
Hope has never ending worth,
Borne to give us second birth.

HOSPITAL FOOD AND NEW BUILDING

Dear Chef of the Day
(Or Clerk of the Works)
We received with joy
Your little jest;
A brick for pud
Which was a treat
Though far too difficult to eat.
We were well on the mend
In peaceful Ward 5
Until we attacked
Your 'Concrete Surprise',
Then out came the teeth
Dented and broke
Trying to eat

Your Health Service joke.
Now we have lock-jaw,
Gums that are sore,
Unable to speak,
We can't ask for more.
When rushed to the loo
From swallowing a morsel
We left our 'deposits',
The 'bricks' and the 'mortar'!
Is this how we play
Our part in the game,
By supplying the builders
Outside with the same?
Next time you cook
Can we please have a hammer
To break up the crust
In appropriate manner?
A fork and a spoon
Are really no use.
Better a drill,
Pneumatic of course!
Then all can appreciate
Your comical works,
As we lay in our beds
Enjoying the perks.

To The National Health: 2040

On Eurotel channel 12 tonight
A documentary showed the plight
Of the Mid Century medical Service.
The Polyblow-structured hospitals
With inflatable research tentacles
Are fast becoming obsolescent buildings.
Body-monitoring cannot be maintained
Due to lack of staff and fiscal difficulties.
Investment in low cost systems stays the same
And preventative medicine will continue
With Repair Banks phased out gradually
Now that people are free
From physical impairment
And deformity.
Delayed conception for the nation
With its teenage sterilisation
Will no longer be compulsory.
Married couples will be permitted,
If proven genetically suited,
To procreate - no more than two children,
If they can pay the Reproduction Tax!
Families with defects are, of course, excluded.
Check your medico-history for the facts.
Free chromosome analysis
And genetic prognosis on DVD,
Computerised for all to see,
Any abnormalities
There happen to be.
Then reversible sterilisation
May be obtained by consultation

With a doctor at the local surgery.
Advice by law and licence granted,
Options of donor cells are offered;
Choice of method, colour, eyes and sex.
The cost is loss of individual privacy.
Tax credits for breast feeding was mentioned next.
For children there will be sugarless sweets
And lollies with fluoride centres to stop decay!
With the latest micro-surgery
Transplants of the kidneys
Using goats, medically
Prepared, are easy.
The plague – the motor car – is finished,
Thanks to the 'Ways of Walking' clinics.
Bicycles and tricycles are commended.
The tasteless soya bean supplement
To our annual meat ration is now
In the range of 'Fibrol 51' foodstuffs.
The shops stock 'Big Tom' new hybrid tomatoes.
Relax with 'Euphori-Q' tranquillisers at home.
Attend the Lister Aseptic Fashion Shows.
Feed your folks Ambrosia, the elixir of youth.
All such slogans of advertisers sell
Products to keep us well.
Radiation treatment cures
Most physical ills.
Schizophrenia, in mental health,
Has been conquered like leukaemia;
Bio-chemical imbalances rectified,
While the rate of suicide increases.

The new Cerebral Activators
For the elderly can stem senility.
The Geriatric Stimulation Centres,
To be renovated for the over-eighties
Will run a new game called "Incontinences".
Life expectancy today is ninety-three years.
Ill health could become the poet's muse
To change the attitudes
Next century of students
In medical schools.

A DIALOGUE WITH MATRON
(On The Death Of My Father)

Who is that imposter in my father's bed?
He looks so ill. He seems half-dead.

It is your father and he is quite dead
He passed away just like I said.

Oh don't be daft. It's a waxwork dummy;
A sick joke I find not funny.

We thought it best to lay him out
In order to allay all doubt.

What happened to his bottom set of teeth?
His upper and lower lips don't meet.

We couldn't fix a smile upon his face
'Cause we found his dentures much too late.

But his mouth's half open like a fish
And he still feels warm and not quite stiff.

It can't be helped, we're short of staff.
To hunt for teeth? Don't make me laugh!

I know that Matron but my father dear
Was much too nice to wear a sneer.

If that's the case, think not it's him
But an imposter of the man within.

I told you so. He is not dead.
That's only his shell upon the bed.
His mask of death looks so grotesque,
At least his soul is now at rest.

BLOW IT

No fun to be abed
To doze and fry
With raging head.

No fun to wake and sigh
As those at home
Leave you to die.

No fun to ache alone
At war with germs
Inside your bones

No fun when eyelids burn
And others gloat
It's now your turn.

No fun a red raw throat
Hot steaming nose
Slit eyes afloat.

Like ice on white-hot coals,
No fun a flu-type cold.

BODY AND MIND

Four score years and one
Is not a lot when looking back.
Body tells another story:
Says its been "a long time on the rack!"

Mind is younger, full of show
While Body's on a 'go-slow';
Wants to replay pleasant times.
Body's not having any of that!

Body, once the dominant part
Demanded urgent needs be met
And like a doting mother-hen
Mind met those needs without a sweat.

Now Time has changed the roles around
And Body is a burden and unwilling slave.

This temple of the soul and spirit,
Worn by the tides on a sea of sin,
Crumbles away with each experience,
While holy chrysalis grows within.

All charity stored and tender reared
To feed eternal life, so feared,
Is kept in Mind, to be released
When lovers once again will surely meet.

The speed of life deceives poor Mind
Who in his prime thought Time was slow.
"Hurry up!"he shouts to slothful Body,
"Time is catching up with us you know!"

A DAY IN THE LIFE

A third of life is lost in sleep,
A third is spent in play.
The fraction left is used up working
The common denominator
Day.

TIME

Time is what we call it by any other name:
Seconds could be minutes,
Hours could be days,
Weeks could be months
And years could be seconds.
Time is, was, and ever shall be
Without beginning, without end;
A cycle of tomorrows,
Todays and yesterdays.
The future becomes the present
Which becomes the past.
Time is first and last.
We make it our servant
But serve as it's slave.
We live hand in hand with it
Until we reach the grave;
Then we are left behind
While time marches on,
Relentlessly.

THE WALL OF TIME

The wise remarks of men made famous by their words
Stand in line upon the Wall Of Time for all to read.
The world looks on, not knowing what the letters say,
For time has passed them by and people rot away.
The words upon the Wall spell out:
"WE LOVE TO LIVE AND LIVE TO LOVE."
So come, forsake all else and you will gain the world
By giving all you have to give.
Immortal phrases scribed by men of old,
Inspired by unknown people, places, things,
Remain when their contemporaries are dead and gone.
We see a part, the whole moves on,
Until the days of Revelation dawn;
When all the mysteries of life shall be revealed
And then the people by the Wall will understand.
All love once lost, the world will mourn.
The Wall Of Time, eternal in its glory, spirals
Upwards to the heavens, winding higher
With ever-increasing circles, it surrounds
The universe of distant sights and sounds;
While senses, mortal, fallible, untrue,
Inform us that the knowledge which awaits
Inside the gates of space, beyond this day and hour,
Is purified with every heart and mind made new.
The path around the Wall is littered with the mounds of bones;
The empty shells of genius once used to build the words
"WE LOVE TO LIVE AND LIVE TO LOVE."

Come, view them from above,
Then shout them out and hear the echo-call.
The Earth may shake, foundations rock,
And all may be destroyed, except
The Wall Of Time, for that will never fall.

LOVE-HATE RELATIONSHIPS

Love

    Respect

        Parents

            Pride

                Fall

Down

    Out

        Count

            Chickens

                Hatch

Eggs

    Fresh

        Break

            Pastures

                New

Desire

    Familiar

        Contempt

            Envy

                Green

Peas

    Split

        Sides

            Opposite

                Love

Hate.

To Tell The Truth

Whate'er I write,
I tell the truth.
You may not like
Whate'er I write.
You look a sight!
Let this be proof,
Whate'er I write,
I tell the truth.

Beauty And The Beast

"You're a beauty" said he.
"And so are you" the Beauty said.
"No I'm not, I'm ugly" said he.
"Then so am I" the Beauty said.

"I love beauty" he said.
"And I love you" said the Beauty.
"Oh, it's not you I love, but your beauty" he said.
"Oh, you beast!" said she.

Lost Love

She did not come.
She said she would
And the hope still
Remains unrealised.

A world unknown
Waits inside me
Trying to escape
Repeated rejection.

A Garden of Eden
She would not enter
And I in turn
Cannot share.

The tender love
I was to give,
And her to me,
Now cannot be.

WHERE WERE YOU?

Where were you when I sought you
Down the darkened lanes at night
And chased your shadow
Up blind alleys?
Were you ever there?
And when I wandered the streets
In hope of meeting you,
Did I really ever see you?
How will I ever know
If what I saw was true?
And when I thought I caught
A fleeting glimpse of you
Among the crowds,
I danced and dodged and bobbed
My way to where you stood.
You were not there;
I found another standing in your place.
Where did you go?
Did you know,
And run to hide your face?
Did you laugh when you saw my tears?
And when I strolled by your house,
Did I see you sitting at your window
Waiting for a sight of me?
Or were you simply there by chance?
And when I cast my eye
In your direction,
Did you want to see me
On the outside looking in?
If I'd stopped and knocked upon your door
Would you have welcomed me within?

Sex, After A Fashion

Evening,
And the sun casts a warm glow
Around the bed
As if tenderly cupping it in gentle hands
Not wishing to disturb the magic of the moment.
Two naked lovers stand spellbound
Wrapped in their own fantasy world.

Outside,
The summer heat rises
From the pavements below
And the room's silence
Is broken only
By the soft cooing of wood pigeons nearby.

A breeze
Enters the open window
And hardens the young woman's nipples
As she waits awkwardly
For the young man's approval.
He reaches out to explore her body
Tentatively, unsure, in awe.

For their blind date each had spent hours
Separately searching through fashionable boutiques
Selecting suitable clothes to meet and greet in.
Now the garments lay scattered across the floor.
First impressions over, pretence abandoned.

In a darkening room
Her head rests on a yielding pillow
And her long blonde hair
Shrouds her heaving breasts.
She opens herself to him, willingly,
Like the petals of a flower
Gathering in the last of the sun.

Eyes wide
He touches her, caresses her, taking in her warmth.
He kisses her smooth honey-set skin,
Tasting her sweetness within,
Absorbing her heady aroma.
'This is sensing. This is possession' he muses,
'This is knowledge of the most carnal kind.'

In the morning,
In a different light,
They wake as strangers
Unable to recapture the magic
Of the night before.
They don discarded clothes from where they fell.
In the darkness of night all seemed well
But dawn has drawn a mist of uncertainty.
Do they go their separate ways
Or meet again another day?
Their bodies move together as before,
As they exit the bedroom door.
Out onto the dusty streets they seek
Even more fashionable boutiques;
Lust to lust their destination.

My Dream Of Love

I love to dream my dream of love
My thoughts my own,
I walk alone
And in my walking wake the sleeping,
Dreaming of my dream of love.

And in my dream I hold no hate,
No anger to suppress.
I talk no less
And in my talking wake the dreaming,
Telling all my tales of woe.

Yet in my dream I do not suffer,
Beseeching those on high
I heave a sigh
And in my sighing wake the dying,
Breathing in my breath of life.

And in my dream I have no heartache,
No passion to control.
I rest my soul
And in my resting wake the living
Praying loud my prayer of hope.

So in my dream I sense no sorrow,
No sadness to be seen.
I live to dream
And in my living wake the loving,
Dreaming of my dream of love.

LIVING FANTASY

On a silent Sunday morning
Slotting thoughts together like a jigsaw,
Forming pictures in our heads.
Heard the sway of way-out music playing,
Softly tapping out a touching tempo,
Urge a time for romance in the bed.
Eyes closed, limbs loose, relaxing;
Floating on a cloud of fantasy.
Smoke filled rings of dreams galore
Drifting through an open door.

Dynamic duo of the avant-garde,
Discover new horizons of sensation,
Explore the furthest reaches of your minds,
Resting as you fall from space.
Heightened senses wrapped in pleasure,
Spellbound by erotic rhymes.
Blindfold, handcuffed, overcome,
Waiting for the climax to arrive.
Muscles twitch and eyes dilate;
Sado-masochistic urges congregate.

Tie your wrists and slap your breasts,
Heave a sigh of satisfaction,
Lift you high and bring me low.
Fingers lightly play upon our flesh
Stirring feelings of desire,
Vibrating memories we hold.
Voyage of adventure nearly over,
New found pleasures duly noted,
Share the moments of elation
Bound together in a revelation.

I'LL DO ANYTHING

Throw me a rubber and I'll rub out my name.
Give me gun and I'll blow out my brains.
Show me the sun and I'll hold back the rain.
Love me today and I'll love you the same.
Leave me tomorrow and I'd die from the pain.
Do what you like I'll take all the blame.
Deceive me, desert me, I'll cover your shame.
Reject me, forsake me, I'll forgive you again.
Ignore me, forget me, my love will remain.

MY GEORDIE LADDIE

I went with my Geordie laddie
For a neet out on the toon.
We had a dance, we had a laugh
We had some Fed and Broon.
Alas the beor was too strong
And he kept falling doon.
My laddie to a netty went
Then said "Ah'll see yes soon".

I went with my Geordie laddie
To St.James's Park one day.
He said it wor a reet good treat
To watch the Magpies play.
Alas the team were all at sea
And threw the game away.
My laddie, he was sore upset
And said he couldna stay.

I went with my Geordie laddie
To the Sunday Market quay.
We stood beside the River Tyne,
He said we'd married be.
Alas, I saw it was nay good,
His heart cried to be free.
I told him so and he got mad
And said he'd go to sea.

I went with my Geordie laddie
To Jesmond Dene today.
We sat beside the waterfall,
The sky came over grey.
Alas, a Da' he was to be;
I found it hard to say.
My laddie said he had nay job
And so he couldna pay.

I went with my Geordie laddie
To his home in Benwell Grove.
He there did vow to spill his blood
But said his seed should grow.
Alas, the Tyne Bridge was the place
And there we had to go.
He planned to jump and end his life -
Then said it wasn't so!

I said to my Geordie laddie
As he walked away from me
"Weor ya gannin hinney?"
And he replied, as if surprised,
"Aam gannin heam hinney!"
I coulda cried.

TRUE LOVE?

He said he loved her
But he left her wild
When she told him
She was having his child.
She told her parents,
They told her to go:
"Go live with your lover,
We don't want to know".

The neighbours judged her,
Said she was a tart.
No ring on her finger,
No hope in her heart.
She went on her way
To live all alone,
No friends or relations
Offered a home.

Now she is a mother
And cares for her son.
She feeds and she clothes him
And they live as one.
No hope to be married,
Her purity stained;
Few men want a woman
Who's second-hand gained.

Take care with the 'letters'
For words can come cheap.
If actions speak louder,
Beware what they reap.
Should sins of the spirit
Be worse than the flesh,
Forgive all our lusting,
May true love be blessed.

ONE AND ONE

I'm so glad to be, I just had to be
Here in your arms.
You're so good to me and your love for me
Shows in your charm.
Way up in the sky the clouds go whistling by
As the tears in your eyes run dry.
You make me want to fly
You take me up so high.
You give me so much fun
You are my chosen one.

I don't like to be, I've no right to be
So satisfied.
You're a dream to me and I love to see
Stars in your eyes.
Way down on the ground the wind goes whistling round
While the love in our hearts abounds.
You make me jump for joy.
I'll gladly be your toy.
You're brighter than the sun.
You call and I will come.

I was slow to see, yet still hope to see
My Wonderland.
Love was dead to me then you said to me:
"Come, hold my hand."
Way over the moon, we'll dance and whistle our tune
When we tie the knot in June.
I'll give you a ring.
Together we will sing.
The bells will all be rung,
Our love songs all be sung,
As one and one make one.

WILL YOU REMEMBER?

Will you remember today, my love,
When you are old and grey?
The words we spoke in confidence,
Our secret trysts for conference?
Will you remember today, my love,
When duty caused delay?
Will you remember
Our first embrace?
Will you remember
The time and place?

Will you remember today, my love,
Should you move far away?
Our kiss-shaped cross of empathy,
The times we shared in ecstasy?
Will you remember today, my love
The songs of love I played?
Will you remember
The way we sighed?
Will you remember
The tears we cried?

Will you remember today, my love,
Should you decide to stay?
Obsessive instincts and desires,
Our mutual bondage, needs inspire.
Will you remember today, my love,
When conscience calls to pay?
Will you remember
How much we pined?
Will you remember
Our limbs entwined?

Will you remember
To look into my eyes
And not despise today?
For it is over, gone.
Our hearts and minds,
Our bodies, souls,
Are now as one,
My love.

Femme Fatale

In darkest night I scanned her sleeping form
Spread-eagled naked on a moonlit bed;
Like Venus in seductive pose, still warm,
Post coital sated limbs like lead.

Glistening in the aftermath of love's exertion,
Her charms abandoned, all aglow;
Lips still throbbing, pout emotion,
Nonchalantly she parts her legs, just so.

I long to touch her succulent flesh
But know she'd take offence at such intrusion;
She would recoil, remove herself afresh,
Declaring my advances all "delusion".

What value then the act of love to savour
When it needs be earned by grateful deeds?
Or granted only as a favour
To those who plead on bended knee?

When one must seek approval to approach
To kindle unrequited love like this,
When every move one makes provokes reproach
What chance is there of wedded bliss?
And yet, as stabbing doubts encroach,
To be at one inside her is my dying wish.

COLD COMFORT

Your body turns cold at my touch.
It's not as though I ask for much;
A little tenderness now and then
Which any cock seeks from his hen.

Why brush me off like a pesky fly?
A needy child would sulk and cry.
Where has all our passion gone?
Where once was much, there now is none.

Age does not wither every need
And what is man without his seed?
Locked in a husk of ageing years
Unable to flee from potent fears.

We close our eyes to future loss;
Like a creeping overnight frost,
We wake to find a winter's dawn
Has numbed the feelings love has borne.

Emotions may snap like rubber bands
Requiring occasional relief by hands.
Treasure the lover who understands,
Who'll bring some warmth to an icy land.

Take A Chance

We, like all the rest, are in the universal melting-pot
Of constant change.
Caught up in a never-ending cycle we cannot contain
Of loss and gain.
Time divides us, time unites us; like specks of dust
Driven by the wind.
How can it be that I should be moved by you?
When did it begin?
Whether by accident or design I do not know
And neither do I care.
Every nerve and cell within this body of mine
Tells me you are there;
The churning stomach, moans and groans away,
The heart-beat races.
My senses, sharpened by your presence, crave attention
Causing chaos.
You live in silence, not sharing your world,
So safe and secure.
No word of comfort nor encouragement you show,
No sign to make me sure.
Shall I but fire one arrow of desire into your heart
And chance disgrace?
'Tis all I ask, to keep me sane, to touch
The beauty of your face.
And when this senseless thing is done in fun
Will you still feel the same?
Or will you laugh it off uncaringly
And view it as a silly game?
I hesitate to test the water lest it be too cool,
In case I catch a chill;

And if the water be too hot then I might harm
The tender roots I've lain with skill.
Could it be that love is leading me away
To live again my youth?
Or am I caught in some cruel trap of fate
To search again for truth?
Experience deceives the memory-banks of fools
Where wasted dreams lie sealed.
Have you the key to open up the safe
To make my dreams come real?
Are you an angel or she-devil in disguise,
Taken human form?
Or are you simply flesh and blood like me
Who needs someone to keep you warm?

SITTING IN SILENCE

I speak with my eyes.
If you look you cannot fail to see
The words I form.
Yet from my lips there is no sound.
A thousand thoughts pass through my mind
As we sit in silence saying nothing.
I sense the closeness of your body
But you do not move.
A mutual deafness fills our ears.
Inhibitions multiply our fears
And in my dreams I feel your tears
Soaking up the emptiness.

Won't you come into my world?
I view it from a distant star
Noting all it's faults,
Yet there is nothing I can do.
I see a million people pass me by
As I sit in silence saying nothing.
I know the pain and tragedy
Of life's lost cause:
As step by step men trudge the highway
Thinking night is day;
They take my world and do not pay
For stamping out its beauty.

All around me people stare
As if I'm standing naked in the sun,
Revealing all I have for them to judge.
Yet I am free and they are not.
Prisoners of themselves they fight for love
As we sit in silence saying nothing.
I sense their open mouths
And vile tongues
Spitting out their poisonous words.
The venom of the suburbs,
Gossip, flies as free as the birds
Feeding on all it can find.

Deaf and mute I watch
As you react to all around,
All ready to conform.
Do you really care what others say?
Are you chained to convention like the rest?
As we sit in silence saying nothing
I share your shame and pity;
Your hopes destroyed
Because you are afraid inside.
Your soul is open wide
For all to see what you try to hide.
Fear not. I will not speak.

Look into my eyes.
I do not have to say a word,
You know my thoughts.
A dreamer in his sleep forgets the time.
Eternal bliss, a lifelong yearning even yet
As we sit in silence saying nothing.
I sense your deep devotion;
Your happy smile
Shines through the window of my heart.
Have faith, we'll never part.
So look into my eyes and make a start.
Look now and tell me what you see.

On Returning

The days apart were long and lifeless
Filled with loneliness drowning fun.
Then the dawning day to reunite us
Rose and set with the afternoon sun.

I returned to find you waiting.
Once again we made for home.
We'd been careless in our caring,
Gone the mystic sparkle once atoned.

My empty heart still aches to be revived,
The love juice of my loins remains untapped.
The valley once I climbed has dried;
My cock-sure confidence been sapped.

Deflated ego like a shrivelled balloon
Waits to find a gust of wind,
To give me life and free me soon
From strings I tied to give me wings.

Ignored, rejected and deprived
By those who do not love me as I am,
Will slowly eat away my pride
And help me die a bitter man.

The golden days we used to share
No longer glow through magic eyes.
Tender touches and sentiments are there
But knowing needs and meeting them has died.

We try to give what we have not;
The reservoirs of love, a desert land.
If we do not communicate our lot
Then ours is but a castle in the sand.

Let's hope this crisis wakes us from our sleep
And lightning flash o'er darkened sky,
To raise us from this compost heap
And open up our half closed eyes.

A New Beginning

We started off as husband and wife.
I believed she was the love of my life,
But slowly she became a sister –
And I really came to miss her.

She cared for me and life was good.
She gave me all the things she could.
She cooked and cleaned and managed by stealth
But less and less she gave herself.

In earlier years the seeds were sown
And for decades apathy had grown,
Then on maturity all seemed lost,
Killed off by middle aged frost.

I prayed and wooed with all my might
Hoping all would once again come right.
Then, I know not how, I know not when
The seeds of love were sown again:
"I'm totally yours" she sighed one night
"I'm here for you, so do what you like."

DYING FOR LOVE

Praise be to lovers who prefer some nookie
To watching tele or eating cookies;
A couple who always want for more
Whether on table, sofa or floor.
As lovers they yearn to taste and feel,
They speak of love, then make it real.

She will bring comfort, peace and accord,
As a lady acting the whore to her lord;
A blessed goddess of human kind,
A jewel to be worshipped, lucky to find.

He will attend to her innermost needs,
Willing to follow whenever she leads;
To kiss and caress her with tender lips
And explore with sensual fingertips;
To nip hard nipples on sensitive breasts
Then blow on them softly in playful jest.

To share such intimate acts and thoughts
Creates a heaven which cannot be bought.
The fruits of their labours lovers employ
Bring years of pleasure for both to enjoy.

Duty not passion may help them survive
For countless years not fully alive.
Neglect and rejection may push them apart
But not if they learn to love with their hearts.
Should they lose themselves and never rue loss,
Should they give themselves and count not the cost,
Then will they have nailed their love to the Cross.

OF HUMAN BONDAGE

"Can I be of assistance madam?"

"What on earth is this
'GUARANTEED ETERNAL BLISS'?"

" It's a sex life not to miss".

"Handcuffs, dildos by the door,
Whips to make your lover sore?"

"Could madam ask for anything more?"

"My God! What have we here?
Plastic, leather and rubber gear!"

"To pacify your guilt and fears".

"Hello! A book about fellatio?"

"Is madam willing to give it a go?"

"Oh no, oh no. I do not think so....."

"How about cunnilingus;
Eating in without the fuss?"

"God no. It would make me blush."

"Is there anything else you'd like to try?
Do crotchless panties please your eye?"

"Thank you all the same, I'd rather die."

"Madam. My shop is here to serve your tastes.
If nothing suits then time we waste.
Let ignorance light your way to grace."

"Sir. Bound as you are in your own dark place;
Any hint of shame there is no trace,
To me you are an absolute disgrace."

"Agreed. We are bound by who and what we are,
By complex and invisible chains.
My custom is to always leave the door ajar,
So please feel free to come again."

THE SACRIFICE

Out of the darkness came the light.
The haze of uncertainty faded slowly away
And vanished with the rising of the sun.
Over was the traumatic night,
Devastated by the bomb of our iniquity.
And slowly a new day was born
Bringing forth hope and newness of life.
Black was the past with worries and torments
Which seemed to grow from nothing
And with monstrous speed matured.
A maze of mental paths our minds did tread
Leading to the road to hell,
Killing all affection, love and trust.
Then quickly came the night
When we relinquished the right
To our declared intent
To live and love, with union blessed.
My paramour and I confessed;
Our selfish acts became the traps
By which we fell as victims
To the atoning sacrifice demanded
For the good of all.

THE PRICE

A word, a melody, a glance,
Can set my tears a'flowing.
Deep in my heart I share with you
The joy of each new time-bought chance
To be with you, united; knowing
That our love will never fade.

Trust me, have faith, do not despair,
Our future hopes bestowing.
The wonders of the world I see
But none to you compare.
I watch; your eyes are moist and glowing.
Be glad, rejoice, be not afraid.

A home; a house without a roof,
But brick by brick it's growing.
Emotions likewise slowly rise
And so remain eternal proof
Of joint affection, always sowing
Seeds of promises we have made.

Two tortured lovers hand in hand;
Outside, cold winds are blowing.
We sit beside the homely fire;
Inside, our flames of passion fanned.
Our burning boats drift on alone, showing
To the world the price we've paid.

Bonfire Night

Guy Fawkes, maverick of British law,
Burning on the seat of Justice,
Surrounded by salamanders
Spitting their lizard-tongued forks of fire;
The fall-guy falls as usual, cremated.
Spirits dance in the pyramid of flames;
Blue, orange, yellow flickers,
Throwing sparks into the sky.
Crackles mingle with the laughter
Of the people standing by.
Children waving sparklers,
Faces shining with delight.
Fireworks banging, popping, fizzing,
Rockets zooming through the night.
Catherine-wheels whizzing round,
Shooting stars falling to the ground.
Silver fountains cascading lights;
Roman candles, red, green and white.
Treacle toffee, parkin, jacket-potatoes,
Consumed like the guy
By the traditional bonfire.

CHARD SUNSET

Glorious glow of the descending sun
With golden puffs floating across
The darkening sky.
Smoke from a garden bonfire hangs
Suspended in a leaning spiral
Tapering to a tip.
Silver bird with vapour trail
Silently sweeps across the copper hue,
Painting an ormolu streak,
Which runs unblended on the horizon.

High above the town
Trees stand to attention, like sentries,
Silhouetted against the sunset,
Guarding the ridge to Snowdon Hill.

To the east, the heavens already sparkle;
Blue-black velvet spangled with stars,
Dressed for night, by a wave
From Tinkerbell's magic wand.
Beneath, in Cathedral silence,
Lies the town in a crystal bowl;
A study of still life,
Lit by the embers of a dying fire.

CHARD 750

Information broadcast in the local press,
Invitations to the party all are sent:
"Come, celebrate this birthday of the Borough,
Join us in this joyous event."

In response we venture out
Through biting wind and flurries of snow.
Family groups with friends and neighbours
Wend their way with heads held low.

'Gainst bitter cold we cling together,
Up Snowdon Hill we climb in darkest night.
The bonfire beacon beams a welcome,
Lighting underfoot the slush and ice.

Excitement, with each heartbeat rising,
Fields now dressed in virgin white.
Crowds assemble round the toll-house;
Hundreds waiting for a light.

Time plods slowly to the nineteenth hour,
While babbling voices reach new heights.
Eager hands hold high the flaming torches;
All seven hundred and fifty now alight.

The maroon goes up, bang on the dot.
The cry goes out, "We're on our way";
Step back to the year Twelve-Thirty-Five,
To January and it's fifteenth day.

Some dressed in medieval garb
And some decked out in fancy dress,
Descend the hill in a river of light
Meandering down to the waiting guests.

Banks of people line the pavements.
Procession flows two thousand strong.
Burning rope and tallow fill the nostrils.
Chard Concert Brass, Pied Piper to the throng.

Bishop Jocelyn first gave Chard it's Charter,
And as we pass the house which bears his name,
I spy a mother with her daughter, injured,
Knock upon the door for help, in vain.

Down, down to the centre of the town we trek,
To the Guildhall with its face washed clean.
The clock tower bell tolls out its greeting,
Spectators cheer and clap and scream.

Majorettes march past with torchlight bearers,
Young and old alike now gathered there.
Upon the balcony of the Guildhall
In the spotlight, stands the mayor.

The festive scene is scanned by T.V. eyes,
Town crier cries "Oyez, Oyez, Oyez."
Pinpoints of light like birthday candles;
One for each year to the very day.

A fanfare shrills the cold night air.
The crowd is hushed, attention drawn.
The chairman of proceedings, Mervyn Ball,
Announces a year of celebrations born.

"Happy Birthday to Chard" we all sing out.
Snow falls like icing on the cake.
Torches are doused like candles blown.
"Let the fun begin with fireworks at eight."

Then after the show and the barbecue,
Like lovers wined and dined and wooed,
We tottered home without a care,
For this was Chard in party mood.
Memories of celebrations, all to share,
Now each can say that "I was there!"

Smoking Ash Tray

Dog-ends of time
In my hands
On my hands
Going up in smoke
Swirling rings of death
Warning of cancer.
Dangerous anti-social
Confidence booster
Acting as a tranquilliser,
Making party conversations.
Lost hands employ
Tanned fingers to secure
Nicotine nerves
With tobacco tar.
Wasting expensive money
In my pockets,
On my conscience,
Addiction.
A health hazard,
Going up in smoke,
Burnt to ashes.

Ash tray
Mother of pearl
Calms the troubled breast;
Sea shell
Rubbish dump,
Flotsam on an ebbing tide;
Crab caught
On it's back
Pecked dry
Hold the dog-ends of my time.

SMOKE SCREEN

You carried on smoking behind our backs,
Our money used to buy each pack.
For many decades you've had your fun
Deceiving each and every one.
A cigarette your closest friend,
Offering comfort, then cancer in the end.
As for us, we count for nought,
Killing yourself without a thought.
You watched loved ones die the same
And yet you play this poker game.
What cause in life ignites your need
For a daily fix of the toxic weed?
Is the love of family not enough
To halt this selfish suicidal bluff?
If only you could face each day and find
Reward enough to toughen up your mind,
Your body then may start to heed
The warning signs which make you feed
Upon the harmful lure of nicotine;
Then the fog of self-deception might recede.

COLIN McGREGOR RAE

On the twenty-fifth of November,
Nineteen seventy four,
At the thirteenth hour,
When the sky was overcast and grey,
Colin McGregor Rae
Breathed in his last breath,
Expired and died.

His wife kept vigil at his bedside
Gripping his icy hand
As the veil came down,
Dividing life from death, night from day.
She had no time to say
"Goodbye", but tired sat,
In silence cried.

Robust and strong but a year before,
A hearty, healthy man,
Suddenly struck down
As if from behind, leaving him dazed,
He clawed his crab- like way,
A convict condemned,
Caught to be tried.

He faced his trial without complaint
And took his tests in hope.
His courage stood firm
For nine long months he survived each day
Between life and death's stay
In purgatory pain
He lied to hide.

He loved his family, home and work.
An ordinary man
Who gave to his friends.
His great pleasure was walking Lyme Bay,
Especially in May.
He spent his birthdays
By the seaside.

He died at the age of forty-five,
When dreams are still alive.
In Axminster his grave is set,
His faithfulness by faith was met.
Whenever I'm on the beach and sight a crab,
Or see ash drop from a fag,
I remember the cancer, the courage and the days
Of Colin McGregor Rae.

Take It Or Leave It

When I am dead
I hope it will be said
" He could write a poem or two";
But when you've tasted three or four
And cannot stomach any more
Perhaps it would be best
To leave the rest
Unread.

Worth

Let nothing mean too much
Or else our judgements pale.
Emotions highly strung may snap
When safety systems fail.

Let not the loss of hopes and dreams
Cause anger or frustration.
Beware ambition when unchecked
By prudent moderation.

Our sense of values may distort
When traumas strike us down.
Such dramas help us all to grow;
Pain has its pleasure found.

Every thing and one has worth,
Relationships are brittle.
Howe'er mundane a moment be,
Let nothing mean too little.

SPINSTER'S SOLILOQUY

A miss by name complete
And missed always by life.
A maiden aunt, a friend, a guest –
Not once a bride or wife.

Evenings I spend alone.
Put out the cat and pause,
Sit down, go round the flat again;
Slippers on feet like claws.

I read armchair romance
About sweet love and flowers.
A virgin's mouth with cups of tea
Sipping away the hours.

I neither smoke nor drink.
I hope I have no sin.
I take no chance at all to lose
And so can't hope to win.

Knitting

Click-click; click-click;
Go the knitting needles
As the grey-haired
Woman rocks in
Her rocking chair
To and fro.
On the wall the clock
Goes tick-tock, tick-tock,
As she knits.
Her mind wanders
As her hands draw
Semi-circles with the wool;
Up and down,
Backwards and forwards.
She is lost in the past;
Memories making
Patterns in her head.
She dreams of the future
Hoping all her plans
Will materialise,
Like the cardigan
She is knitting.
Click-click; click-click.
And time ticks by
As the clock
On the wall
Goes tick-tock, tick-tock.

HANDS

Flesh
Bones
Blood
Nails
Digits
Pick up
Put down
Move around
Make a sound
Open wide
Try to hide
Throw aside
On a limb
Right and left
Inside out
Tell-tale lines
Reading palms
Join together
Making signs
Moving
Hands.

STEPPING OUT

One step
Out of the black void
To a mass of gas cloud.
One step
To explode
To form a sun star.
One step
Spun off the sun
Like clay from a potter's wheel
To harden to a planet.
One step
When the Biomagician
Cast his spell
To produce an amoeba.
One step
To flip a fish
One step
Out of the sea,
Ditched on a beach
And a freak to survive.
One step
To a reptile,
Cold blooded and ugly.
One step
To a mammal,
Warm hearted and cuddly.

One step
To a Homo sapien.
One step
To fly in outer space.
One step
Into a black hole for eternity.

INERTIA

Many
A
False
Step
Has
Been
Made
By
Standing
Still.

DESTINATION UNKNOWN

I came only to
Say that I cannot
Stay.
I'm so lonely it's
Time I was on my
Way.
People are strange
And they don't like to change
Unless they can have their way.

If you need me you
Only have to give the
Word.
If you want me I'll
Fly back swift as a
Bird.
Things are the same,
Like the sound of a plane,
And the words we've already heard.

I feel empty and
That I cannot
Deny.
You have plenty and
I know the reason
Why;
You take up a man
And you get what you can
While there's nothing money can't buy.

No point in stopping
When everything's rotting
As we drift slowly apart.
Like ships in the night,
We pass by the light
Of the moon, in the dark,
Destination unknown.

Getting Nowhere

                    stop.

            full   I

       a   feel

    to   I

come   am

I   going

   time   round

      each   in

          circles

It's A Boring Routine

It's a boring routine
Getting dirty things clean.
Every day it's the same
Till my lover comes home again.

Monday morning,
Get up in plenty of time,
Get the kids off to school
In a bit of a rush.
Got to get the washing out
On the line.

Gather the clothes,
Hoping the weather stays fine.
Do the shopping in town
In a bit of a rush.
Got to get the washing out
On the line.

Washing machine
Hums and gives me the sign.
Throw in the dirty old clothes
In a bit of a rush.
Got to get the washing out
On the line.

Into the dryer
Which spins and makes a whine.
Take a trip out the back
In a bit of a rush.
Got to get the washing out
On the line.

Monday evening
My lover comes home on time.
Get the kids off to bed
In a bit of a rush.
Then bring the washing in
Off that line.

It's a boring routine;
Well you know what I mean!
Every night it's the same
When my lover comes home again.

THE KNOCK UPON YOUR DOOR

As you sit and ponder in your
Semi-detached suburban home,
Do you ever wonder why
You live at all?

Washing the dishes, cleaning the floor,
Darning and mending,
Do you stop
To answer the knock upon your door?

As you relax in your favourite chair,
Head back and cool,
Do you ever wonder why
You live at all?

Watching the tele, reading a book,
Hoping and praying,
Do you rise
To answer the knock upon your door?

As you take off your clothes
And prepare for bed,
Do you ever wonder why
You live at all?

Making a meal, checking your change,
Scrimping and saving,
Do you run
To answer the knock upon your door?

As you lay awake beneath the sheets,
Your body limp,
Do you ever wonder why
You live at all?

Feeding your child, wiping the tears,
Caring and tending,
Do you need
To answer the knock upon your door?

As you eat your breakfast
In the early morn
Do you ever wonder why
You live at all?

Cleaning your shoes, leaving the house,
Rushing and cursing:
Do you remember
The sound of knocking on your door?

No one is there.
Your lover in despair has gone
And you were the one
Who ignored
His knocking on your door.
His heart is cold
His love is dead.
And you,
Who walk along the street
All dressed to kill,
Do you ever wonder why
You live at all?

When You Are Bored

When you are bored
Let time stand still and think a while
Of me and of love stored
In these few words, which with a smile
You may reflect upon and know
That I am with you when you're bored.
Let time pass by and fill your mind
With thoughts of love sweet absence finds;
For love is life and life renewed.
Remember this when you are bored
With nothing else to do but brood;
For I am with you, love restored,
Till time betwixt us is no more,
And here I sit, right by your side,
For love, it knows no law.
And so as always I abide,
In thought and word, with you,
This moment... when you're bored.

No Exit?

Where, oh where is the exit to this treadmill
In which I voluntarily grind away
The very roots of my existence?
Trapped in a grip of strenuous effort
Which drains the very blood which drives me on.
Flat out I rise again and run.
My God, is there no respite from this plight?
Is there no saviour meet to help me leave this state?
If only I could be arrested by those most dear
And led away to havens of their own, I'd yield;
And gladly would I surrender all my world
Which clings to me in mortal fear.
For when the stones beneath my feet
Are ground to dust,
Then will the sinews of my mind and body
Collapse exhausted, spent and bust.
Those who thought me happy at my wheel
Will say "didn't he do well?"
And yet, outside myself I need to be;
To dance and sing and play about,
With little children run and shout,
Then fall about with glee.
Oh when will this solitary sentence e'er be cut
By someone else's will?
Must I toil in torment endlessly
While others watch admiringly?
Am I stuck for all eternity
So helplessly, with people,
Who like owls in daytime,
Cannot see the need in me?

IRON BARS

You are the magnet
Me the lodestone.
There is an attraction
Though we are poles apart.
When we are together
We each repel.

Travellers together
On life's journey,
Like railway lines
We never join but run parallel
Until we reach
The end of the line.

We need each other,
Locked in our cells
Of solitary confinement.
Alone, and sometimes lonely,
Members of a chain-gang
Bent on survival.

Underworld Coming-Out Party

Convict Number 453
Coming out after a seven year stretch
Emerges through the postern
In the tall spiky gates
On the stroke of nine
Free!

Welcoming warmth of the morning sun
Eclipses the sojourn duly done.
Caged bird, wings unclipped,
Eyes agog, flies off
Free.

Underworld party planned in his honour,
Awaits the prize thug on release.
Sent down for G.B.H.
"Knuckles" Case runs wildly
Free.

Rejoicing friends with pleasure prepared
The villain's sexual feast.
His bottled up frustrations pop
And fantasies flow
Free.

The young blond virgin of his choice is raped
And crooked needs by deeds are met.
The brute in a frenzy
Cuts Agnus Castus down
And 453 at last feels
Free!

No Salvation

Pity the man who feels no sorrow.
Pity the man who feels no pain.
He is the man who will die tomorrow.
He is the man who will never live again.

Man On The Cross

Long, long ago, a carpenter's son
Cut all his ties with his home and was gone,
Wandering around in the heat of the sun
Carving his name on the hearts he turned on.

He questioned his elders and punctured their pride.
Their power and position he chopped down to size.
They waited to bait him, to trap him they tried,
But none could avoid the look in his eyes.

His friends were the poor and deprived of his day,
The outcasts and driftwood of death and decay.
He helped them to burn all their props and to say
"This is the life" and "This is the way".

He loosed all the chains for all men to be free.
Their hang-ups he hung on that Calvary tree.
They crowned him with thorns and mocked him with glee.
"Betrayed by a kiss, king of love, come and see!"

"Oh why were you dying, man on the cross?
Why were you crying, 'lema sabachthani'?
Did you think God would save you, not leave you be?
And how did your blood from the nails set us free?"

★ 'lema sabachthani' means 'why have you forsaken me?'
in Aramaic, the language Jesus spoke.

MISTAKES

The Romans crucified a man
Because the Jewish authorities
Accused him of claiming to be their king.
He said he was the Son of God.
Was he genuine, deluded, or a fake?
I'd love to know,
Because either he or they made a mistake;
And mistakes can kill
Both the body and the will,
Even of the innocent.

Heaven

Is there a place somewhere above
Where dwells the Maker in His might,
Now growing old and white with beard,
Sitting, watching us below;
Patiently waiting, ever ready, quick to strike,
Guiding His flock by day and night?
Is this what we call 'Heaven'?

Is there a state of mind or being
So well defined, so near to bliss,
In which our senses reach nirvana;
So sharp, so sensitive to beauty,
Consciously growing more aware that this,
Like some supernatural kiss,
Is what we call our 'Heaven'?

It cannot be.
The first mocks God by making Him a man;
The second by making Man some kind of god.
Perhaps the answer lies somewhere between the two,
Or where they both do meet and merge as one?
Either way, I cannot find my 'Heaven'
And if I could, I think you'd find it hell.

In Hell

I am broken,
    I am a shell.
I am empty,
    I am a well.
I am dying,
    I am a cell.
I am unlovable,
    I am in hell.

No Need For Salvation

I don't want to be saved;
Not as I am,
Not as a man.

Eternal life must be boring;
All that time
Which would be mine.

I don't want to sing with angels;
I'm tone deaf.
I'd prefer to rest.

I wouldn't mind being God;
That would be fun,
For everyone.

We could do what we liked;
Do our own thing,
Create anything.

I would need unlimited powers
To build a heaven
I could be happy in.

Even then, I'd take it for granted
And get bored
With it all.

Nuclear Power

A speck slits the blue
Silk of sky slowly falling
Like a dart to earth.

People cowering
Watch with fearful eyes praying
For a miracle.

The missile hangs in
The air above the quiet
Cathedral suspense.

A dot hits the ground
Frozen in a streak like an
Exclamation mark.

Full-stop silence as
Petrified parents think last
Thoughts before the flash.

Brilliant white hot
Light too bright to face hides the
Growing mushroom cloud.

The blast-rush of wind
Scorches eyes out of sockets
With its kiss of death.

Somewhere a puppet
Psychopathic push-button
President half-smiles.

PROPHET OF DOOM

Believe me, I don't deserve this fate;
I walk through woods of hollow trees,
The earth is damp beneath my feet,
I'm cold inside and hungry.
The birds no longer sing.
Silence lingers in the air.
The babbling brook is dry.
The sky is black with cloud.
The path is paved with rotting leaves, for
All is dying.

The corn is brown, unharvested.
Flora by the wayside withers and droops.
The sun has gone, there is no light,
Covered are the woods by night.
Cold misty air, so sharp,
Rises from the ground.
No sign of life I see.
Deserted, the woodland waste
Decays outside the city gates, for
All is dying.

Leave me. It is already far too late.
The city streets are empty
And all is quiet.
The doors are locked and bolted.
No welcome greets a stranger passing through.
The echo of a woman's cry
Fades away as eyelids close.
No children playing,
No preachers praying, for
All are dying.

I slump beneath a blackened tree,
It's branches brittle bare.
The landscape is so desolate
It stabs my throbbing head.
Pains like arrows strike me quick,
I reel and dizzy
Have a fit.
While numbness floods my brain,
I too am feeling very sick as
All are dying.

My crooked smile splits bloated lips
As rain runs down the stricken tree.
Large acid drops and water drips
Are gently soaking all of me.
No shelter anywhere.
Am I the only one alive?
Has God deserted all of us?
This is no Eden, more Armageddon.
The land is flat and even
I am dying.

I kiss the ground on which I crawl.
The grass turns slowly black.
The skeletal trees are cracked.
Above, the thunder roars in triumph.
As lightening flashes down the barks
The hollow trees ignite,
Like torches in the night,
Giving out a warning glow
To anyone who doesn't know, that
All is dying.

Leave us you devils of mankind
Who torment us with your lust for power.
It is you who lead us to the brink
Of what might be Earth's final hour.
Time and time again you fight
For what you see as so-called might.
You fill our futures full of dread,
So do not mourn for me if you are left
And I am right, when all is dead.
This world is slowly going insane;
Our final hope must surely be
That one day Christ will come again.

DEAD LOSS

On Judgement Day
It will come as no surprise,
Bulbous-headed Priapus and I shall rise.
All in vain if you ask me;
Neither male nor female
At the Judgement
Will there be.

Unexpected

Watch and pray
Night and day.
Who can say
When he will come?

He said he would come back again
To judge the living and the dead,
With power and great glory
As King of Kings and Lord of Lords to reign.

Every eye shall see him.
Suddenly, everything will change.
In the twinkling of an eye,
Some will live and some will die.

Like a thief in the night
He will come at an unexpected hour.
Was he wrong or was he right?
Only time will tell if he has God's power.

So watch and pray
Night and day,
Lest he catch you sleeping
In your disbelieving.

TREAD SOFTLY

Where gods are,
Men fear to tread
In case they too are trodden on.
Even gods without legs
Are to be feared,
For they can tread on you
Without your knowing;
Until the weight of their burden
Is felt too late,
As you wander through the mire
Going your own way,
Searching for the gates
To Paradise.

GLASS DOORS

Shamans, medicine men, witch doctors,
Prophets, priests and seers
Sought to impose order and system
On the scattered arrays of chance,
Interpreting their meanings by ritual and dance.

Oracles and soothsayers,
Guardians of the supernatural,
Passed on their secrets of divination
To the chosen few who were their protégés,
Thus retaining status and honourable patronage.

Now powerless to lock their doors,
The keys to which they hold no more,
Augury's realm of secrecy is smashed
By knowledge winged in the shape of glass,
Cut by reason on a distant shore.
Accessible via the Internet,
Such powers are open to all.

TAKE MY SOUL

Sunshine and showers
Keep coming to
Colour the flowers;
Bees humming as
Church bells in steeples
Keep ringing to
Call all the people,
Birds singing to
God in His glory
Telling the story of love
Which has come from above.

Words in the Bible
Keep saying of
Life " It's a cycle";
Men praying in
Temples of Satan,
Keep leaving to
Search for their Maker;
Hands reaching to
God in His glory
Telling the story of love
Which has come from above.

Creatures of Nature
Keep dying by
Others who hate them;
Mass crying while
Armies of martyrs
Keep bleeding to
Death for their daughters,
All leading to
God in His glory
Telling the story of love
Which has come from above.

Lord be in my mind.
Teach me to be kind.
Lord be in my heart
And make a start;
Make me new, make me true,
Make me whole, take my soul.

KING ARTHUR

King Arthur was of lowly birth
He was by Merlin made.
Tintagel Castle was his home
And fighting was his trade.
He fought the Saxons and the Scots,
He sought the Holy Grail.
He held his court at Camelot
With knights so bold and brave.

King Arthur was a Cornishman
And noble were his aims.
He ruled with Guinevere his queen
And for her beauty paid.
He fought the Irish and the Danes,
He sought the Holy Grail.
Merlin made him a magic sword,
Excalibur by name.

King Arthur beat his enemies
And never made them slaves.
He taught them justice with his sword
And freedom freely gave.
He fought the Romans and the French,
He sought the Holy Grail.
His knights were faithful, but alas
Was by his wife betrayed.

King Arthur went away to fight
And left his queen to reign.
His nephew Mordred came one night
And with the queen did lay.
As soon as Arthur and his knights
Were told the sorry tale,
They journeyed home to save the throne
And Mordred he was slain.

King Arthur took a mortal wound,
His body racked with pain.
They carried him to Avalon,
His life they tried to save.
His queen sought refuge as a nun,
He sought the Holy Grail.
The Cup of Christ he came to sup
Then rested in his grave.

BLIND FAITH

When I walked for the blind and their charity
Down through the valleys and over the tors,
The sun shone brightly on all before,
And the blind in their night showed a light to me.

Contrasts in Nature displaying disparity
Reflected the walkers who followed the cause,
When I walked for the blind and their charity
Down through the valleys and over the tors.

With love in their hearts they helped me to see
How blind was my faith in God and His lore.
Down through the dales and over the moors
I saw that they could so easily be me,
When I walked for the blind and their charity.

THE WAY

Since she is too blind
To find her way, I would pray:
"Lord, forgive this child
And lift her to thy bosom
So that she might see the light".

ABRAHAM

Abraham was a man of faith.
Abraham was a man of grace.
Heard the call of the Lord
"Better go and leave this place,
Without a word".

Abraham left the City of Ur,
Took his wife, his goods and hers.
All the family and their friends
Took their camels, flocks and herds,
Without a word.

Abraham obeyed the Lord,
Trusted in his guiding hand,
Wandered through the desert plains,
Made his home in the Promised Land
Without a word.

Abraham was a man of faith,
Made the father of the race.
Heard the call of the Lord
"Abraham, Abraham, you'd better go,
Without a word".

CHANGE

Life is good,
Full of love;
From above
Comes all we need.
Times are so easy,
We tend to forget.
I wish you'd believe me,
You'd have no regrets.

If you stay
You will pay
For the day
When all is gone.
Don't be so dreamy,
You don't have to yawn.
Change is so easy,
Wake up to the dawn.

Like I said,
You'll see red
If you're dead
When all arise.
Don't be so greedy
With money and power.
You may not believe me,
But now is the hour.

You must change,
Or be changed.
Cut those chains
From off your feet.
Who is the master,
Who is the man,
We follow after,
Best as we can?

ZODIAC RHYMES

Aries the Ram
He stole some jam
And gave himself a treat.
The ram he fled
From farmer Fred
Who cut him up for meat.

Taurus the Bull
Thought life was dull
So bought a china shop.
The bull went wild,
In came a child
And smashed the blooming lot.

Gemini Twins
Made such a din
And quarrelled every night.
The twins they fought
Till they were caught
Then argued who was right.

Cancer the Crab
A man did grab
Out swimming in the sea.
The crab squeezed tight,
The man took flight,
"You're tickling me!" cried he.

Leo the Lion
He bought some iron
And built himself a cage.
The lion did roar,
He'd lost the door,
"I can't get in!" he raged.

Virgo Virgin
Gets in a spin
When faced with something new.
The virgin cries
She always tries
But finds "new" hard to do.

Libra the Scales
Shouts " heads" or "tails"
According to the rules.
The scales go down
Holding the crowns
Of honest men and fools.

Scorpio the
Scorpion the
Sexy, sinister thing.
He bends his back
To hide the fact
His kiss is like a sting.

Sagittarius
Gregarious,
An archer and a beau.
He twirls his curls
To slay the girls
With arrows from his bow.

Capricorn Goat
Stands by and gloats
When others take a fall.
The goat is rough,
He thinks he's tough
But listen to his call!

Aquarius,
Precarious
Water-carrying man,
Plods to and fro
Then stubs his toe
And falls into his can.

Pisces the Fish
Pose on a dish
And drink to pass the time.
The fish can't wait
And eat the bait
Until they catch a line.

ASK THE DEAD

Ask the dead to tell the future.
Babylonians, Etruscans, Greeks, Romans,
Aztecs too –
Practised haruspicy
To interpret the will of the gods.
Sacrificial offerings
Of fish, sheep, oxen and frogs –
Humans too –
Carried on their entrails
Cryptic clues and messages.
Even the death-obsessed Egyptians
Possessed recipes of rituals
For necromancy;
Reanimated corpses
And conjured up spirits
Helped them believe
In supernatural powers.
Time has obscured our view
Of the gods of yesterday.
Spirit mediums, ouija boards
And planchettes
Are all we have today.

SACRED MUSHROOM

Sacred mushroom make me a meal.
Hector's nectar helps me grow.
Atlas Mountains reach for the sky.
Mighty mushroom, tell me why.

Mandrake magic let me feel,
Pawing flesh so silky soft.
Satan's servant bound to die,
Mighty mushroom, tell me why.

Fate-plant of the open fields,
Nature's servant of the womb,
Teaching men to live and die,
Mighty mushroom, tell me why.

Countdown to destruction, flash of fire,
Burn the flesh-plant of desire.
Sow the seeds to raise a lie.
Mighty mushroom, tell me why.

Dust to dust my destination;
Ego-tripping god of revelation,
Who is the A and O of I?
Mighty mushroom, tell me why.

EARTH, WATER, FIRE AND AIR

Earth is soft and fertile;
A bed in which grow seeds
Of grain, flowers, weeds and trees.

Water is wet and flows;
The source of life and power,
It creates and destroys at will by the hour.

Fire is hot and burns;
It transfigures and transforms,
Ashes to ashes and dust to dust.

Air is invisible all around;
It is free for us to breathe,
Both still or moving at gale force speed.

The earth needs water
And the fire needs air.
Nature needs them all, so I should care
While I am still here, that they are still there.

CLOUDS

Clouds,
Shifting, drifting
On cushions of air, floating
In a fantasy world
In a Freudian head
Well hidden.

Clouds,
Moving, soothing
Great vapours of mist, cooling
Shapeless amoebic masses,
Changing abstract patterns
On blue sky.

Clouds,
Heavy, earthbound
In depressing cells, falling
From damp decaying walls,
As monotonous drips I reach
Out to touch.

SKY

Above the clouds, a dazzling sun
Accentuates every hue of blue.
Below, mountains of moisture ascend in thermal puffs
Like seas of candy floss, bubble and stew.

Nimbus, frothing crests rear higher,
Curling themselves into cannonballs
Which Thor projects with a mighty roar
While gilt-edged and silver linings grace their fall.

Sky, battlefield of the spinning Earth;
High over heads where feral winds sway,
Among temperatures too cold for birth,
The triumphs of men may be blown away.

HEAVY SHOWER

Footsteps splattered like fish
On the stone pavements of the streets.
People hunched and huddled,
Darted for refuge from the sheeting rain.

I nestled in a doorway
Mesmerised by the rhythmic beat:
Pit-a-pat, pit-pat plop.
Drips dropped from the gutters overhead.

My skin bristled up in waves
As I lolled snug and content.
Water gurgled down the drains
And gushed spluttering from broken pipes.

Bright neon amber street lights
Cast a warm glow over buildings.
Walls and roof-tops shimmered;
A new look, fresh sheen, bestowed on everything.

As the deluge subsided
And floodwater ran off in streams
Fast disappearing underground,
I felt a slow wet trickle down my neck.

Storm In A Tea Cup?

Cumulus cloud accumulates
And water droplets form
Heated by the burning earth
Brewing up a thunderstorm.

From drought to flood and round again
Such crises loom and leave.
Then people pour their troubles out
By brewing cups of tea.

Western Man

In Western Man there is an urge to rationalise
The mystic powers of Nature wherever he can;
Equally, we see the instinctive need to nationalise,
                              In Western Man.

From the realities of the unseen world he ran,
Hiding in countries he worked to industrialise;
Shedding childlike reverence, sacred awe, for
                              "Scientific" plan.

Sophisticated modern aids dimmed his orthodox eyes
To the invisible mysteries of life he once scanned.
Now he is blinded by the loss, leaving much to materialise
                              In Western Man.

Concrete Water – Creeping Urbanisation

Rows of roof tops on the skyline
Shrouded in mist,
Like waves on a sunless sea,
Eroding the shoreline,
Advancing silently.

Earth mounds, ridged for development,
Clouded in dust,
Like ripple marks on the sand,
Reshaping the beach
The tide has reached.

Roads cutting through the countryside
Banked by hovels,
Like rivers running into oceans
Attacking the landscape
Flooding escapes.

GRASS ROOTS

Friesians frozen on a landscape
Black and white on green.
Mamma mammals tapping pastures
Farming full of cream.
Devon milk and money flowing
Liquid paper round,
About the lush sleep of the suburbs
Floats a fluid sound.
Rattling rows of golden bottle tops
Wake dozing herds of flesh;
In glass houses pint-sized cows
Partly pasteurised fresh.

Inside a home at mother's breast
A baby seeks a nipple.
On heated stove the food of love
Simmers to a ripple:
Man cooing, cow mooing.
Outside, wet grass grows brittle.

This vision of a winter's morn
Fades with watching weathered eye.
While home delivered milk is mourned
Mounds of concrete and brick sprout high.
Panoramas blotched by angled roofs
Blot verdant fields blood red.
New livestock in designer boots, not hoofs,
Trample underfoot with careless tread
Young shoots of grass once free to spread
Which now lay waste beneath grey stone beds;
Ground on which fresh human herds are bred.

FACE THE NATION

The face of England
Blotched and blighted,
Struck by the Architects' plague.
That face which once was
So beautifully made
Is pock-marked with cities
And inflamed conurbations.
Villages and towns like festering sores
Expand with the economic need for more.
The stain of industry everywhere,
Spreading poison, disease and grief,
Like eating away the leper's cheek;
Eyes smarting, nose running,
Ears aching, mouth gaping,
Skin cracking, oozing pus,
Smeared with the ointment 'Pollution'
(A product marketed by Evolution)
To hide the parasites feeding off the nation.

Oh, Merry England weep no more!
Have a face-lift, find a cure.
Smile again with conservation
Or pay the price, decapitation.

Heads And Tales

The wide oceans,
The high mountains,
The trees in the woods,
Have stories to tell –
If only they could.

The leaves on the trees,
The fish in the sea,
The birds in the sky,
Have tales to tell –
If only they'd try.

The rocks on land,
The desert sand,
The flowers in bud,
Have stories to tell –
If only they would.

Clouds in the air,
Waves on the water,
Spray in the wind
Sweep over my head
Telling their tales
In a howling gale.

The Four Seasons

Young lovers strolling hand in hand,
Children playing,
The days stretching longer,
Buds bursting forth,
Rain showers with the sun breaking through.
Shadows becoming stronger,
Lambs gambolling in the fields;
Great patches of greenery unfold
As the clouds roll back
To reveal the Spring.

Colours and flowers abound in glory,
Crowds jostling,
Lazing in country fields,
Garden barbecues,
Sunburn lotion and sultry nights.
Salad and fresh fruit for meals,
The stillness of a heat haze,
Sweat running off the brow,
All juices flowing fast,
Rising to salute the Summer.

Shrivelled and shrinking, growing old,
Leaves falling,
Nature's back is bent.
The biting wind, howling,
Grey skies and lashing rain
Hustle Autumn to retirement.
Paint peeling off the window ledge,
The days, like steps, becoming shorter.
Bodies running out of steam
Cannot keep up the pace.

Ice on the pond, thick fog and frost;
Snowflakes drifting;
A cold deserted landscape.
Old age creeping;
The living, sleeping-death of hibernation.
Brittle branches break
Like bones on skeleton trees.
First signs of resurrection show;
The robin on the garden gate.
And Winter once again recedes
In deference to Spring.

ALL SAINTS, KIRKBY MALLORY

Come, let us congregate in communal joy,
To celebrate this great Festival of Flowers.
Let All Saints be filled with lavish songs of praise
And old church bells ring to herald God's hour.

Man born of woman full of noise and woe,
Be still! Hark the silent witness of the flowers!
They toil not to adorn themselves in splendour
Nor don crowns of pride to advertise their power.

Rejoice in their richness and abundance of blooms.
Like our own frail flesh, holding goodness within,
They flourish then wither, colours slowly fade,
The pleasure they give, unstained by man's sin.

Flowers carved in cedar wood embossed in gold
Adorned Solomon's Temple, symbolically sound:
Tokens of victories, remembrance and love;
Gifts we can honour on Byron trod ground.

Feast eyes and keen senses on hues by the score,
Variety in texture, fragrance and line;
Each one unique like the family of Man.
There is much to be gained if we give them our time.

FORGET-ME-NOTS

Why do you glide
Through my dreams day and night
With such effortless ease?

Is your image
Branded on the membrane
Of my mind for ever?

Will each new wave
Of memories erase
Our love letters in the sand?

Will the red bricks
Which housed our passion
Fall and fragment with time?

On a cleft stick
I show the cloven hoof
And reveal my true self.

Your deft fingers
Which fondly boxed me in
I curse with vitriol.

With cynicism
I see a wheel turning,
Inventor forgotten.

Fate was his name
And I, Cyclops declare
The circle breaks the square.

Beware frail flesh
And biased lustful eye,
Of forget-me-not sighs.

REMINDERS

Christmas
Suffering Slave
Promised God incarnate
Born a babe into Bethlehem
Star-struck.

Easter
Resurrection
Branch of Jesse pruned so
New buds can grow and blossom on
Life's Tree.

Whitsun
Quickening wind
Fanning flames of passion
Transforming embers into white
Hot coals.

All Souls
See the future;
For the future is death,
Omnipresent with life and as
Awful.

FLOWERS OF YOUTH

Flowers of youth in our good land
Rise up and catch the morning sun.
Gently fold it in your hands,
Keep it with you and have fun.
Take it before the evening comes.

Flowers growing in the sunshine
Stand up and kiss the air we breathe.
Sparkle with your budding minds,
Softly open up your leaves.
Caress the sad and lonely breeze.

Gentle flowers of youth begun,
Colour our world as we pass by.
Meadows made for you to run,
While waving to the distant sky
Taking the clouds of tears to dry.

Flowers of youth be strong and brave,
Face up and slay the common foe.
Knowing love will always save,
Take it with you when you go,
Before the winds of winter blow.

COLOUR

If what I saw was brown
And you saw it as blue,
If we both knew it as pink,
Would you take it to be true?

If we were all colour-blind
And colours were not real,
Would it prejudice our outlook
Or change the way we feel?

COLOUR BLIND IN '59

A member of our Commonwealth
A Britisher like me
Arrived in England.
He tried to find a house or flat,
Somewhere to stay
But the problem was his colour,
It was black.

We advocate equality,
We teach it in our schools.
Equality for all.
Some people slammed their doors at that,
No room for more.
The problem was his colour,
It was black.

At last he found a place to live,
The landlord called it 'home'.
A tiny room.
The walls were soaking front and back,
But never mind,
You paid a little extra
Being black.

He found a job to pay his way.
His education sound,
His word his bond.
There was nothing that this man did lack
Except one thing,
For when it came to colour
He was black.

The white man had his pride to keep,
The black man had the same
But not his freedom.
The neighbours never called him "Jack"
They called him "Coon".
The reason was his colour,
It was black.

God made the races four in all:
Pink, yellow, red and brown,
Bestowed with love.
He blessed them all, the world to pack
With mortal souls.
There are no colours
White or black,
So racists you've been told.

COLOUR TELEVISION

Most people have a television;
Most with colour, a few without.
(Artists tell me there are no such
Colours as black and white.)
Each colour T.V. has so many lines
Which you cannot see
But together form a picture,
On a screen in the corner,
Which we commonly call 'the tele'.

It dehumanises every form of life
And develops our tolerance of horror;
Of man's inhumanity to man.
Everything is edited and re-edited
And the bits remaining
Are joined together and sent out
For us to consume as we wait
Like dustbins to be filled
Sitting at home watching 'the tele'.

Colourless conversation and discussion;
In the pub, at work and at home.
People with screened vision and imagination,
Unable to think for themselves,
Who are content to vegetate, ask:
"Did you see 'Horizon' or 'Panorama',
'Man Alive' or 'World in Action'?"
They argue all the issues
Saying "It said so on the tele".

It's true that colour adds life and realism
To the pictures on the screen and
To the lives of those who cannot get about.
But even those blessed with colour T.V.
Still see aspects of life in black and white
And swear blind that what they believe
Must be right, and what they see
Must be true, without a doubt,
Because they saw it on 'the tele'.

News In Papers

News is now;
Tomorrow it is history.
News is facts;
Though misleading they may be.
News is people;
Who, without the how or why.
News is action:
Wars, murders and disasters.
News is fun:
Pin-ups, babies, sport and stars.

News is photographs and words.
News is 'REAL' (with a question mark).
No one argues with a camera
When it flashes light on dark.
Different headlines, different meanings;
Captions tell us what we're seeing.
Not for the reader to decide.

The news of our times
Arrives with the mail
Express fast.
Guardians of truth
Mirror the facts
About the people.
Biased observers
Telegraph tales
As we bask in the sun
And read about our favourite star.

IT PAYS TO ADVERTISE

It HELPS ME to sell the product.
A simple formula
To motivate the buying public.
Appeal to their need for

Health,
Efficiency,
Leisure,
Pleasure, or
Security. If that doesn't work, try

Modernity or
Economy.

Create the need
Provide the product,
Sell the idea,
Advertise.
It may not help you
But it HELPS ME
To take the money out of your
pocket
And put it in mine.

THE CHARMER

What words would you like
To hear me say?
I say whatever pleases
Other peoples' ears.
It pleases me to please them.
They like to be teased.
To be pleased
By me and my words.
They think I'm such a pleasant fellow
But my words are just words;
Hollow words,
Which sound nice to the ear,
To those who are near.
I am a fraud, a dummy,
A mouthpiece only
Few can afford,
Programmed to please.

I perform with effortless ease,
Without thought,
Without meaning
Without shame.
It's all a frivolous game
And my aim doesn't matter.
I more than influence to deceive,
More than flatter,
More than persuade.
No need for me to batter
My willing victims into submission.
At the end of the day
I always get my own way.
"Oh, charming!"
I hear you say.

THE END OF PRIDE

Bands of light flash blind the eyes,
Across the mind a thought inscribes
A memory; a vision seen, interpreted
By knowledge gained from past experience.
Corrupted, our innocence turns black.
The swollen grains of crops become
So large that senses, cold and numb
Give out: the harvest been and counted;
The autumn leaves in loose-knit piles, ignited.
The fires of hell released to fly
In gusts of wind which light the sky
Bright red; the golden dusk diluted,
And colours run before bleary eyes, unblended.
The crooked road of life bends back
The bones of those who lack the strength;
The anguish on the face, disjointed,
Becomes a mask of doom undaunted.
Where freedom grows the dove descends,
The shackles of time transcend
All glory; the proud who worked to win promotion
Find in their death no self-approbation.

MR. JONES

Mr.Jones smokes all he can.
His skin sports a nicotine tan
Which people think he gets on the Riviera.

Mr.Jones speaks with a stammer
Since his daughter, with a hammer,
Hit him between his legs around Cape Horn.

Mr.Jones plans well ahead.
He bought his wife a double bed
Because he did not like her sleeping on the floor.

Mr.Jones sits in his corner
Playing with his doll called Norma
Which, with heated breath, he inflates from time to time.

Mr.Jones delights in malice.
He bought an old pretentious palace
With the rent money extorted from the poor.

Mr.Jones sits on his throne;
A second hand loo, all his own,
Made of gold he charges visitors to view.

Mr.Jones worships all he owns.
He lives in a million different homes
Wherever love of money is to be found.

Mr.Jones has even changed his name
Because it sounded rather plain.
Now he answers to the name Smyth-Jones.

SENSES

Touch tells me you are here.
I can feel the shape of your body,
The warmth and smoothness of your flesh.
It tells me the air you breathe has motion.

Taste tells me what is bitter and sweet
When I drink and suck or eat.
I can taste your salty tears
And the fruits of your desire.

Sight gives colour to my life;
It brings proportion and perspective.
My eyes take pictures of your face
To store away in my memory album.

Smell distinguishes animal
From vegetable and mineral.
I can smell the fragrance of your hair
And the odour of your armpits.

Without hearing I would not know sound;
I would not hear the music in your voice
Or your knock upon my door,
Nor the rustle of your dress as you pass by.

There is a sixth sense which no one can define.
It makes us conscious of other things
The given senses can't detect.
Maybe the most important one of all?

We also have a sense of humour and of honour,
A sense of what is right and wrong;
A sense of achievement and responsibility,
A sense of our own importance and ability.

If all our senses worked towards a common goal,
Would the end result in common sense?
And yet with all our senses open to deception
How can we be sure of anything at all?

Our senses tell us what there may be
And where, and when, and how;
They do not provide any key at all
To why we are here, locked outside the door.

HAIKU
(BEYOND OUR KEN)

Things exist which we
Don't hear, see, smell, taste or touch;
Our sixth sense says so.

Orange Tang

Orange juice
Morning marmalade
Buttered toast
Breakfast round the table.

Sunshine trees
Spanish greengrocer
Jaffa world
Growing sweetly pliable.

Orange squash
Afternoon serenade
Quenching thirst
Pip-throats warmly viable.

Sunset fruit
So health refreshing
Caked in taste
Rolls in tacky palms.

Peel the skin
Suck the vitamin
Blood-red mouth
Releases the balm.

At First Sight

That first glance,
That first spark,
That surge of pure elation;
Desirous to possess such beauty,
Such perfection in another.
Like a miracle of Nature,
Difficult to comprehend,
Or reason How? or Why?
The welcome in your eyes,
Your luscious lips
Which softly mouth "Come in",
Invite a confident response,
Positively charged.
Then to find our bodies faultless fit
To form a channel
For our unadulterated lust
Through which great tidal waves
Of passion roar
Like the Severn river's bore.
To fall in love, so commonplace,
Requires a special time,
A unique face,
For that first glance
And that first spark
Which quickens the heart.

Gradually, over time we learn
That falling out of love, in turn,
Is just as easy.
For relationships to last
We need to study what has passed.
Love is neither falling in nor out,
But 'doing' is what it's all about.
Commitment is an act of will.
Caring, a duty to fulfil.
Immature, our " love" is wild,
And lust alone is not enough
To raise a child.

EYE OPENER

We meet again,
On waste ground.
Hopes rising,
The blood rushes
In gushes
Through blue veins.
Thunder pounding
Round my head.
Dilated pupils,
Suns eclipsed
Peer out of
Burning eyes.
Behind us and out of focus
Lies the debris of past desire.
Silent messages transmitted,
Received, recorded and replayed
Quicker than the speed of light,
Form a million impressions.
My eyes blink, uncertain.
The flesh on your cosmetic face
Seems to be creeping, weeping,
And falling in blobs to the earth;
Image destroyed in a stroke,
I see you for what you are.
I turn and rush for the waiting bus
As a bent coin slips from my pocket
And rolls away into the gutter;
Useless, worthless, lost for good,
Never to turn up
Again.

GLASS EYE

I stood by a pool, dazzling,
Like a window of glass
Reflecting the sun.
I looked in the mirror
Beyond the surface
At the cool depths below,
Where I saw darting fish
And plant-like forms
Swaying to and fro.
Each in its own way
Searching for food.
But for all I could see
The water was void.
A drop from that pool
Of clear water I took
And placed on a slide.
Then I had a close look
Through a more powerful
Mechanical glass eye.
And there, invisible before,
Were many strange creatures
Swimming about.
Without a doubt
There are more,
Micro- and macroscopic,
Which remain to be seen
Through the windows of life
By the 'blind' human eye.

BOA VISTA

The island, a " Boa Vista", that's for sure;
Atlantic rollers thundering in from the west
Exploding on the soft white sands along the shore,
Expending energy till they come to rest.

A "Good Sight" for sailing vessels seeking shelter
Trying to outrun dangerous tropical storms.
Early years saw cattle raised while shepherds sweltered
Under a blazing sun too hot to grow corn.

Later, the English came, extracting salt from sea.
Then others produced ceramics and cloth to trade.
Today there is tourism; beaches, palms and turtles free;
A source of wealth for modern day pirate raids.

This once peaceful virgin island paradise
Has become a noisy hedonistic Mecca.
While the constant breeze quells thirst like ice,
Screaming children overheat and adult thieves turn wreckers.

Westward on the distant horizon line
Rests Penwith, now glass clear, now smudged in haze;
A granite peninsula, dark, remote,
Like a watching finger marking time.
Across Mounts Bay, flash red and white rays;
The eyes of Wolf Rock searching out boats
Around Land's End, down a coast of Serpentine.

Behold! Kynance, showplace of the Lizard,
With its manifold elaborations;
The Gull Rock and Asparagus Island;
Black rocks colour-washed like witch and wizard;
A cove, steeple pierced with incantations,
Rainbows of spray above floss-silk sand.
It's beauty fretted by winter blizzards.

Behind, bulked large, the headland of the Rill:
A tableland's edge, whence first was sighted
The coming of the Spanish Armada.
Before, sits Lion Rock, with looks to kill,
Guarding the cove and cliffs, his mane blighted,
Head turned, watching the sea and its saga
Beneath the ridge of Yellow Carn, quite still.

Inland, to the north, are the war-stained downs,
Where airfields scar and slice both hill and heath.
Predannack, Goonhilly and far Culdrose
With tumuli and furze in stoney ground;
Land most holy, enchanted, wild and bleak
Now house a heliport, saucers and roads;
Solitude shed by the droning of sound.

East of the Lion, the scarf of Pentreath,
A sweep of sand against fierce cliffs' wall,
Brushed by the foaming surf of man-high waves.
Yet Pentreath is a plain and tranquil beach,
The most romantic and charming of all,
Where adders bask on hot summer days
And men go a'launcing on moonlit trysts.

Below our window, the end of the lawn,
Where cropped grass topples into barley fields
Which slope to the sea to the south and west.
From here we see vessels Atlantic born
And pass away as the sea-sky yields.
Of all panoramas this is the best;
Large ships and small boats parading from dawn.

Southward, the land falls to old Lizard Head
And a vast arc of luminous green sea.
Beyond are The Stags and old Man o' War;
Great stones out of sight, dark reefs for the dead.
Rocks to which only Shags and Cormorants flee.
A coastguard lookout hut above the shore
Acts as medic to a constant deathbed.

A little below us along the road
Beside Maenheere where a Tricolour waved,
On the first morning of Armistice Day,
A Belgian widow and daughter abode.
The husband drowned but his parrot was saved;
Some say the shock made the parrot turn grey.
What happened to them is no longer told.

Down farther yet to narrow Rocky Lane,
Sunk between bramble, boulder and high fern;
And on, beside squelching trickle of stream
To Pistol Meadow, of mounded square fame,
Where two hundred souls, from legend we learn,
Were washed ashore and then buried in seams;
Men of war felled by the Rock of that name.

It is said hordes of dogs raced to the scene
To eat the bodies cast up from the wreck.
Hundreds of firearms and cannon were found
But wreckers soon came to pick the place clean.
Don't go at night if you value your neck.
It is haunted and eerie, odd without sound,
And many strange sights are said to be seen.

Cross over the stream where tamarisks hang.
Step up the steep weedy stairs to the cliff
Which leads to the least troubled Lizard cove.
Behind us the seaweed camomile tang.
Ahead, the old lifeboat station and slip,
Polpeor, where Tennyson bathed, I'm told,
And on to the southernmost point of land.

About us, a chain of bright brimming pools,
The spatter of pebbles and sand on shore,
The incessant wash and drag of the tide,
A natural arch, a cavern for fools.
Gullies, clefts, coves, caves and rock-falls galore;
A coastline dragon-green monster waves ride
Breathing white fire, crested with silver, they rule.

Eastward, the lighthouse lime washed dazzling white,
Directs the liners, oil-tankers and boats
Away from the booming cannon-fired sea.
Its beam like a tongue, licks the skyline night,
Silently warning anything afloat
Of treachery beneath, on bended knee;
The beam like a sword at the Old Head swipes.

Return along lanes meandering back
Past Penmenner House, now only a wraith,
Down an arras of fuchsia draping stone,
Where wallflowers roof the rough gravel track
Beyond feathered plumes of tamarisk waifs
To the house "Kynance Bay", once Trewin's home.
Views around here the rest of Cornwall lacks.

CAN YOU NOT HEAR MY WORDS?

Your beauty blinds me like the blazing sun,
I cannot look you in the face;
I stand mouth opened wide, struck dumb.
Can you not hear my words?
Is this the time and place?

Whispered greetings, dispersed in confined spaces,
I want to speak and tell you all,
But mute I am for fear of my disclosure.
Can you not hear my words?
Can you not hear my call?

Temptations play upon my mind.
I wait for you to care.
My passion, frightening to behold, is blind.
Can you not hear my words?
Consumed with lust, beware!

My heart and mind are torn in two.
To hold your hand is all I ask.
Such emptiness of soul, I never knew.
Can you not hear my words?
Hold on, I will complete the task!

We meet from time to time, a fleeting glance.
Do I detect in you the same emotions
Flowing through you in some ritualistic dance?
Can you not hear my words?
Come listen to my sweet devotions.

Silent as the night and deep in thought,
I wonder if you really know;
My secret hopes remain at nought.
Can you not hear my words?
Love takes a time to grow.

Gentle is the breeze and softly falls the snow.
I kneel upon the ground in silent prayer
Offering thanks, at last you know;
You've heard my silent words
And now I know you care.

LIVING LANGUAGE

Language is a life-long sentence for Man,
Made up of letters, words, paragraphs
And chapters of communication,
In the ever-open pages of the
Book of Life;
Punctuated only by illness
And death.

A Written Proposal

Shy thoughts on surface paper dwelling,
One probing pen to poke them into life.
Wild words can do their business stirring strife,
Making yet breaking tension; doubts dispelling.

A rush of tears to eyelids welling;
A careless phrase may cut us like a knife.
Shy thoughts on surface paper dwelling;
One probing pen to poke them into life.

In a world where literacy is selling
And the use of written words is rife,
Dare I take the plunge and beg you be my wife?
Shy thoughts on surface paper dwelling;
One probing pen to poke them into life.

FOR YOU MY LOVE

For you my love, words from my pen will flow for ever,
Scribing time-eternal thoughts which may seem clever.
Come to my side and sit with me, fair maiden still.
You are my hope for helpless is my will.
There is a reason for the twisted tortured way I feel;
I'm just a dreamer, I cannot comprehend what's real.
There is but one journey's end to each upon the earth;
Our bodies are a'dying from the moment of our birth.
So when the testing comes, I'll stay your fears,
Stand firm throughout and shed no mournful tears.
And when the raging storm has passed you by,
If you should turn and chance your eye,
You'll find me standing by your side,
For love-found moments never die.

TYPING

Typing is writing
Mechanical fashion
Letters in fetters
Released by the hand.
Notions in motion
Float across keyboard
Passing from mind
Into matter in bands.
Ribbon well hidden
Printing black words,
Posted to people
In far-away lands.
Carriage release
And carriage return,
Round paper bail
Shifting its stand.
Rivers of figures
Flooding the page
Ripple the surface
Channelled by man.
Typing like writing
Is tiring and testing
Hard on the hands
As scouring black pans.

Away With Words

Restless hands entwined,
Thumbs touching palms
Pushing buttons, stirring desire.
Your knowing looks and comic glare,
Those captive eyes which mesmerised,
Causing heads to turn and stare.
Warm hands cupping my unsure face
Focusing my attention.
Soft fingers gently ploughing through my hair
Slowly soothing away all cares,
Creating furrows straight and true
Sweeping worries from the air.
A waft of breath upon my neck
When cuddled up against the cold.
A familiar tap on wrist or arm,
The times you stroked my inner thigh,
Stoking lust to further highs.
Signs and signals, thoughts untold,
All these and more I miss,
With no last chance to say 'Goodbye'
Nor seal our loving with a kiss,
No words can tell.

END OF STORY

I was always an open book
Simple to read,
Transparent.
It was always in your look
To find a host
Who'd give you the most.
As I am quick to believe
You thought me easy to deceive,
But my trust was broken
When the first lie was spoken;
I knew then I would only grieve.
Never once the first to hug
Or offer me a lover's kiss,
You spoke only of material bliss.
Yet always keen to respond in kind
To whatever others had in mind
You gave yourself freely
To anyone touchy-feely.
Hidden secrets tucked away
Never to see the light of day,
And yet I did indeed perceive
What time itself has proved-
Very sad but true,
I never really knew you.

The Artist And The Mirror

The artist deals in what is truth and what is not.
He shows us what he can of life
By hanging up a mirror on the wall.
The glass, sometimes distorted, does not change.
People look and read and listen;
Gleaning what they may from what
Is spoken, seen or sung or written.

The artist is a teacher and he teaches what is real,
Reflecting life in all it's many forms
By hanging up a mirror on the wall.
The wall revolves and images appear.
People look and read and listen
Hoping they can see themselves in what
Is spoken, seen or sung or written.

The artist observes the world in which he lives
Creating new impressions for the inner eye
By hanging up a mirror on the wall.
The framework varies in size and depth.
People look and read and listen
Drawing false conclusions from what
Is spoken, seen or sung or written.

The artist, inspired by generosity and love,
Offers help to those who want to live
By hanging up a mirror on the wall.
He projects himself unwillingly, though
People look and read and listen,
Believing they can share his life from what
Is spoken, seen or sung or written.

The artist is a man apart, destined to suffer
The indignities of a martyr
By hanging up a mirror on the wall.
He gives himself to his calling, while
People look and read and listen
Knowing not the meaning nor the mysteries in what
Is spoken, seen or sung or written.

The artist proclaims his message to the world
Communicating all he possibly can,
By hanging up a mirror on the wall.
He hates the artificial, unoriginal or false, but
People look and read and listen
Passing superficial judgements on what
Is spoken, seen or sung or written.

COMING TO TERMS

My parents confessed I was an accident
Conceived amid bombs at the height of war.
They already had three. Didn't want any more.

They said they would have preferred a girl.
They liked the names Rosalind and Rose,
To suit a wished-for scholar or lover of prose.

In fact my talents lay in the field of sport.
No family members ever came to watch me play;
"A grammar education going to waste" they'd say.

When I 'got religion' I applied to be ordained.
I quite fancied being a padre or a preacher.
The Church denied me, so I ended up a teacher.

My wife would wish me to be a practical man;
A maker and mender, helper and cleaner,
Not someone who spends his days a dreamer.

I have two lovely irreplaceable daughters
But always yearned for a companionable son.
I was told that three is unlucky for some.

Let nothing mean too much when testing Fate.
It's said that those who want will never get;
Like when we pray for sun it turns out wet.

Desire and denial, with familiar ring,
Resonate throughout our capricious lives.
Not a thing about which to rejoice or sing,
Just a warning bell; the toll of Future's sting.

THE ONE AND ONLY

On my journey home
I passed by way of Laugharne
And there
Along the Cliff Road
I came upon a boathouse
Where for fifteen years
Until his death in '53
Lived the "one and only"
Welsh bard.
Alas
I could not enter
The garden nor the house
For the cost
Was more than I could raise.
I consoled myself
By taking in the panoramic views
Across the estuary of the Taf
As he had done
A thousand times before.
I wandered back
Along the lane
And found the simple wooden shed -
His sanctuary -
Where he had written
Millions of words
With poor reward
Which still survive
Though he is dead.

Further on along the lane
A man
Well on in years
Was seated on a wall
Resting from his brushing up
And hedgerow cutting.
As I passed by
He smiled
And greeted me
A cheery "Good day".
I stopped in my tracks.
He touched his cloth cap.
I replied in kind
And asked if he knew
The way to the grave
Where the great man lay.
"Aye" said the old man,
"I knew him well, poor boy.
Such a nice boy he was too.
Used to walk down this lane here.
Saw him almost every day.
Moody he was too.
Sometimes he'd be full of the joys of spring
And stop and pass the time of day.
Talk for hours he would.
Other times
He'd pass by
And ne'er speak a word.

Shy, see.
Sensitive too.
Pity he had to die
To be famous.
When he was alive
Never had two pennies to rub together
He didn't.
No…
All that business
About him being an alcoholic –
Absolute rubbish, see.
Never had enough money for drink…
All a myth.

Oh aye.
'Twas the drink that killed him though.
Drank a bottle and a half of whiskey
So they say.
Would have killed the strongest man.
Only thirty-six he was too.
Nobody ever heard of him
When he was alive.
Then they started coming
In the summer
After he'd gone.
Pilgrims.
Now they come
Summer and winter
From all over the world.
Had a girl of sixteen here the other day.
Come over from Canada
She did.

Said she hitch-hiked all the way.
No wonder there's so many murders about.
Ask for it
Some of 'em do."
He leaned on his walking stick
Bent like his legs
Riddled with arthritis.
His big brown eyes
Moistened a little
As they stared at me
In vacant expression.
"Aye" he muttered
As if to himself.
"Pity he had to die like that
To get famous.
Buried in the churchyard he is
Out on the St.Clears road.
If you go that way
On your right
You'll see St.Martin's church.
There's a car park there.
You'll find some steps going up.
Go up the steps
And 'cross the bridge.
There, on the other side
In the centre of the field
Is a simple wooden cross.
Painted white, it is.
Surrounded by great marble tombstones
In memory of others.
It's the only wooden cross there.

Too poor for a proper headstone, see.
That's where you'll find
The one and only."
I thanked the old man
And he shook me by the hand.
"Aye" he sighed
As I went on my way.

WITHOUT RHYME OR REASON

Where is the poet for the common man
Who will use common words
To describe the common lot
Of common men?

Where is the poet for the ordinary man
Who uses ordinary words
To express ordinary feelings,
And ordinary thoughts
With ordinary meanings?

Why do poets arrest the passer-by
(Searching for a common heritage),
With minutiae extraordinary,
Babbling from their ivory towers
In Babel?

Gone the style to deal with abstract ideas
Head-on.
Gone the love of poetry
Which died
Unwon.

Found, the extraordinary man
For the common poet;
Found, the muses for the elite
And self-elected audiences.

Now you tell me:
Where is the uncommon poet
For the common man?

Myself

I'm inclined to be good and inclined to be bad.
I'm usually happy but sometimes I'm sad.
I try to do good but so often I fail.
I'm undoubtedly witty, but my wit can grow stale.

Some call me a fool, others say that I'm wise.
I'm probably both but they don't realise
The fact that we're all a little of each.
Perfection is something quite out of our reach.

They say I'm eccentric, it's true I can tell.
One moment in heaven, the next I'm in hell.
I tend to be cautious and common with sense.
I'm very understanding, but sometimes I'm dense.

Occasionally, I'm stupid and very unwise.
I'm usually honest but I sometimes tell lies.
I'm very observant and seldom forget
The moments of pleasure with people I've met.

I'm extremely obliging, respectful and kind.
I never shoot dogs or people who are blind.
I'm very considerate as you can well see.
Although I forget things, I've a good memory.

Independent, yet faithful, and loyal till the end,
I'm a perfect companion to stranger or friend.
Yet proud and conceited, I'm humble and low,
Sarcastic and lazy, untidy and slow.

I'm a likeable person as everyone knows;
Me, most of all, as each moment it grows –
My liking myself that little bit more –
Good on the surface but bad to the core.

A Simple Man

I am a simple man at heart
Who enjoys the occasional fart;
For farts are fun and simply made,
Pure air their pungent smells pervade.
Some are silent, others loud,
Some disperse a gathered crowd.
Unique in pitch as well as pong
I like them more than any song.
When in the bath we liberate
And bubbles blown reverberate.
When bursting forth in packed out room
They break the boredom or the gloom,
Causing folk to glance and titter,
Keen to see who has the jitters.
Light a match and you will find
A blue flash leads to burnt behind.
Guilty party flushed with shame
Departs head down to fart again.
To those uncultured in the Arts,
The most expressive is to fart.
To a simple man it's all too plain,
No two farts are e'er the same.

LIFE'S JOURNEY

I remember I crawled with limited sight.
When I was a babe I was vaguely aware
There was much more to see from high in the air.
When I was lifted I glimpsed for a time
Horizons far distant, great heights to be mine.

At length I stood up and finally walked.
I saw the world from a much higher plane
With risks and gambles you find in a game.
There were trees, high hills, steep cliffs, above all –
Social ladders to climb from which I could fall.

I longed for the day when I could proceed
To ascend the mountains, their beauty to view.
The world diminished the larger I grew,
So I set my sights on goals I could reach
And believed I had the world at my feet.

As an adult I ran with abandoned haste.
Intent on my goals I missed much on the way
Yet some things I saw which remain to this day.
The journey, so easy at first sight appeared,
Proved longer and harder than ever I'd feared.

Meandering on, my progress was checked:
Obstructions, delays, disasters and loss;
Deep gorges, steep slopes, swift rivers to cross.
Companions I joined gave help and good cheer,
My hardships though shared, grew harder each year.

A kind word, a smile, a wave on the way;
At last a breather gave chance to look back
To see my children retracing my tracks.
What once was so near now seemed afar off;
One rests more often approaching the top.

My legs wore weary towards journey's end.
The panorama clearer, nearer the peak;
New challenges proved more difficult to meet.
I saw the mistakes which I made in my past –
I wasn't the first and I'll not be the last.

The sun which sets in the warm western sky
Will rise in the east at the breaking of dawn.
With night drawing on I must wait till the morn,
Then the summit I'll reach and take in the view.
On the other side await pastures new.

Watching The Sun Set

The Sun
  is setting
The Sky
  is darkening
The Air
  is chilling
The Mist
  is rising
The Birds
  are silent
The Trees
  are still
The Lovers
  are sleeping
The Day
  is over
And I am
  one step nearer
My Journey's
  End.

LAST ORDERS

Grieve not for me when I am gone
But fill your heart and mind with song.
Mope not nor hang your head for long
But gird your loins and journey on.

Our bodies were not made to last.
I'm stuck with mine until it's ash!
For me the future is now past.
What of my soul? I dare not ask.

Remember me, a part of you;
Hand in hand we stretched and grew,
Bonded by values shared by few,
Weaned on love in a family pew.

Be thankful for each gifted year.
Rejoice and hold each moment dear.
Treat death itself as nought to fear
And wipe away all mournful tears.

We march through history marking time
And one by one drop out of line.
Your turn will come just as has mine
So celebrate your life in kind,
Enjoy my wake, fine food and wine.

POSTSCRIPT

It is unfortunate that there is a great deal of intellectual snobbery surrounding poetry and a lot of nonsense spoken about it. While there may well be a place for abstract ideas to be expressed in abstract forms my work falls at the other end of the spectrum. I use more verbs than adjectives. My own feeling is that poetry should be solid in structure and more direct in the management of ideas. Many of my poems are intended to challenge people's ideas, beliefs, habits, customs and general mores of present day society; to get them to think about everyday matters in a different light. I suppose they are largely 'teaching' poems in one form or another. Even the many poems dealing with different aspects of love, as well as many of the narrative poems, have a question mark hidden in them somewhere. It is not the job of an educator to provide his students with all the answers but to teach them how to ask all the right questions. I hope I have succeeded to some degree through the medium of poetry.

M.J.C.

ACKNOWLEDGEMENT

I wish to say a big thank you to everyone at Troubador Publishing for all their help in bringing this venture to fruition. In particular Jeremy Thompson for his encouragement and facilitation; Amy Statham for her patience and forbearance and Sarah Taylor for her diligence and for going that extra mile.

Also many thanks to all the family and friends for their help and advice in the early stages of preparation of the the manuscript, especially to Dorothy Bambridge, Richard Butlin, Josie Gatley, John Hind, Maris Hind, and Joan Wedgwood. Your views and comments were much appreciated.

Lastly to Fairport Convention, Steeleye Span, Dire Straits, Seth Lakeman and many others who accompanied me along the way without knowing it. To one and all, my heartfelt thanks.

In Memoriam

My forefathers were born, lived and worked on the Royal Estate, Sandringham. My grandfather was a head chef in the Royal household and also kept wicket for Norfolk. I was named after my uncle James Alfred Cook who was the Milk boy on Sandringham Farm. He enlisted in 1914 as a Private in the 1st/5th Battalion of the Norfolk Regiment and was killed aged 19 in action against the Turks in 1917 at Gaza in Palestine where he is now buried in the Gaza War Cemetery. R.I.P.